T0384253

Corporate Strategy (Remastered) II

Since the onset of the Fourth Industrial Revolution numerous corporations have found that traditional 'strategic planning' is ineffectual in responding to, or capitalising on, unforeseen or unexpected change. In recognition of this and associated symptoms of inertia, bankruptcy or worse, this fieldbook was written for the purpose of guiding strategy practitioners through their intended or unintended journey into the future by providing meaningful strategy practices that enable responses to disruption and more importantly, better strategy practices overall. With a focus on strategy practice ('doing' strategy), this book represents a 'how-to' of Third Wave Strategy as defined in detail in the introductory book *Corporate Strategy (Remastered) I*.

In addition to a description of methods that contribute to the philosophy of Third Wave Strategy, readers will witness the experiences of a virtual illustrative company that is travailing the same journey of organisational transformation and renewal that the methodologies described in this book also seek to address. The overall value of the book, therefore, is its ability to relate theory to practice in a factual and experiential format.

A key part of the use of the virtual case study based on the illustrative Third Wave Industries (T-wI) Corporation is the blending of the system and process mechanisms that are a part of Third Wave Strategy and its framework, the strategy tools and techniques that are drawn from new and existing strategy practice and the soft issues that are represented by the human responses to change, as well as the management of change enacted in a corporate environment.

Paul Hunter (DBA) is Founder and CEO of the Strategic Management Institute (www.smiknowledge.com) and past partner at PwC. He works on a global stage consulting and teaching. He is also the author of *The Seven Inconvenient Truths of Business Strategy* (2014) and a chapter contributor in *Corporate Universities: Drivers of the Learning Organization* (Rademakers, 2014).

Corporate Strategy (Remastered) II

A Fieldbook Implementing High
Performance Strategy and Leadership

Paul Hunter

Routledge
Taylor & Francis Group

LONDON AND NEW YORK

First published 2021
by Routledge
2 Park Square, Milton Park, Abingdon, Oxon OX14 4RN

and by Routledge
52 Vanderbilt Avenue, New York, NY 10017

Routledge is an imprint of the Taylor & Francis Group, an informa business

British Library Cataloguing-in-Publication Data
A catalogue record for this book is available from the British Library

Library of Congress Cataloging-in-Publication Data
Names: Hunter, Paul Wilson, 1954– author.
Title: Corporate strategy (remastered). II, A fieldbook implementing high
    performance strategy and leadership / Paul Hunter.
Other titles: Fieldbook implementing high performance strategy and
    leadership
Description: Abingdon, Oxon ; New York, NY: Routledge, 2020. | Includes
    bibliographical references and index.
Identifiers: LCCN 2020005843 (print) | LCCN 2020005844 (ebook) |
    ISBN 9780367473204 (hardback) | ISBN 9781003034827 (ebook)
Subjects: LCSH: Strategic planning. | Leadership.
Classification: LCC HD30.28 .H86823 2020 (print) | LCC HD30.28
    (ebook) | DDC 658.4/012—dc23
LC record available at https://lccn.loc.gov/2020005843
LC ebook record available at https://lccn.loc.gov/2020005844

ISBN: 978-0-367-47320-4 (hbk)
ISBN: 978-1-003-03482-7 (ebk)

Typeset in Bembo
by Apex CoVantage, LLC

Contents

Figures

Tables

About the author

Paul Hunter is a highly experienced management consultant, educator and business executive. He is the founder and chief executive of the Strategic Management Institute, www.smi knowledge.com, and a former managing director of an independent management consulting firm. Prior to establishing that entity with his colleagues, Paul was a partner with a global management consulting firm. Before entering consulting, he worked in industry in a finance and accounting capacity. He commenced the consulting stage of his career in Indonesia where he was based for approximately two years.

A key aspect of the management consulting and education coursework presented in this book is the content developed as part of the thesis that contributed to his award of a doctor of business administration degree. Paul is a former office bearer and paper reviewer for the international Strategic Management Society. He has worked with numerous global corporations in both consulting and executive development roles. In addition to this book, he has co-authored professional practice papers and given presentations in many seminars, briefings and conferences addressing a diverse range of audiences. Examples of more recent publications and speaking engagements follow:

Publications:

> *The Seven Inconvenient Truths of Business Strategy,* Routledge, Oxon, UK, 2014.
> **"Raising the Bar at Mars University":** A case study and chapter in Rademakers., M. *Corporate Universities: Drivers of the Learning Organization,* Routledge, Oxon, UK, 2014.

Singapore Management Review: Co-author of "Contemporary Strategic Management Practices in Australia" and "Back to the Future, Strategy in the 2000s".

Quoted in *BRW* magazine and contributed blog post to *Leading Company*, an online magazine.

Strategy Survey: Strategic management practice in Australian organisations in collaboration with Swinburne University.

Presentations:

Smiknowledge and Strategic Management Institute International Conference: "*Strategy as the Enabler of Change in an Era of Unbounded Disruption*", held in Melbourne in October 2017 and London November 2017. www.smiknowledge.com.

Strategy Workshops in Tehran: Appeared as the guest of the Iranian-based Strategy Academy.

Strategic Management Society: Presented in October 2017 in a conference in Houston and November 2006 in a conference in Vienna.

CPA Australia: Presentations at CPA Australia conferences, including CPA Congress in 2010 and 2013.

Chartered Institute of Management Accountants UK: Presentation in Manchester, 2017.

Institute of Directors UK: Presentation in London, 2018.

Conferences:

ANZAM: Paper presentation in 2005 titled "*The Conduct of Business Strategy in Australia*".

To contact Paul, email him at smi@smiknowledge.com, or join us on LinkedIn: www.linkedin.com/groups/3762509/. I look forward to hearing from you.

Introduction

What to do when you *can't be what you can't see*

Consistent with the scientific nature of organisational behaviour, strategy is grounded in social, rather than technical, science. It's appropriate, therefore, to equate the success of a youth development program with measures of success in business. In her book *You Can't Be What You Can't See*, McLaughlin (2018) describes how an after-school youth development program gifted disadvantaged youths from Chicago in the mid–1980s with an ability to see and appreciate a pathway to a life that they could have only imagined previously. Key to their salvation, McLaughlin (2018) discovered, were the three factors of *mentoring, exposure to activities and resources beyond their neighbourhood*, and, *a culture of belonging*.

Translate this into a context of corporate high performance, and the factors of success could read as follows:

Mentoring: a strength of strategic leadership and focused organisational learning
Exposure: reframe and be prepared to adapt to unseen change and invest in the invention of deliberate, potentially disruptive change
Belonging: broad-based Stakeholder Engagement and open management practices

We propose in this book to provide you with the means to 'be what you can't see' and thereby enable you to realise a state of personal and organisational high performance.

Concept of Corporate Strategy (Remastered)

It's difficult to relate to a future that quite literally can't be seen or predicted. Managing through that difficulty has been the sole objective of corporate strategy since the Ancient Greek generals (strategos) first started plotting strategies for war. *Corporate Strategy (Remastered)* represents a reworking of one of the earliest forms of corporate strategy that was conceived by author Igor Ansoff in the mid–1960s and still survives today. In our remastering of strategy, our intention was to evolve an integration and enhancement of Ansoff's early concepts with new and advanced strategy concepts. In the development of our remastered program, our objective has been to develop, understand and reinvent. Accordingly, we sought to make strategy relevant and meaningful in a new world order brought about through the disruption created by the Fourth Industrial Revolution (4IR) and revolutionary changes in societal attitudes, local and global politics and the physical environment.

In taking the concept of corporate strategy into its next iteration, it was an honor to acknowledge and applaud the 'lighting of the fuse' that Igor Ansoff (1965) initiated through the publication of his book *Corporate Strategy*. Representative of *first wave strategy*, the notion of corporate or strategic planning gave rise to numerous developments in strategy and strategic thinking; these are recognised by us as evidence of *second wave strategy* practices. Similarly, the remastered version is referred to as *Third Wave Strategy*. Cognitive aspects of Third Wave Strategy are conducted through the enactment of organisational learning, the practice of structured and critical strategic thinking and a culture of openness and engagement. Physical aspects are grounded in the construct of a system-based, fully integrated Strategic Management Framework, now known as a Third Wave Strategy framework.

How to use this book

This book provides insight into the notion of a remastering of strategy. Presented within a context of Third Wave Strategy, the objective in its writing is to explore, with you, methods of strategy practice, which will lead to a corporation's capacity to transform to an elevated state of high performance. Although written by a single author, Paul Hunter, it is his preference to acknowledge the work of many contributors and participants in his coursework from which this, and the companion *Corporate Strategy (Remastered) I* book, is based. Accordingly, Paul prefers to use the terms 'we', not 'I', 'our', not 'my' and 'us', not 'me'. Some of the individuals to whom Paul owes a debt of gratitude for their contributions are Anthony Claridge, Mike Donnelly, Stuart Orr, Stephen Pitt-Walker, Gaye Mason, Greg Baker, Andrew Brown, Steve Perera, Fred Davis, Phillip Lange, Martijn Rademakers, Dianne Kelleher, Laurence Gartner, Noordin Shehabuddeen, Greg Trainor, Alexie Seller, Paul Foley, Nick Price, John Cockburn-Evans, John Toohey and Denis Bourke.

As a fieldbook, it delivers content supporting an experiential workshop-based program that explores a systems approach to strategy practice from conceptualisation, formulation and implementation through to alignment. Its purpose is to explain, expand and demonstrate the application of Corporate Strategy (Remastered) to practice. Both this and the companion introductory book, *Corporate Strategy (Remastered) I*, can be used to conduct the associated facilitation/action learning workshops and consulting projects. Our experience has shown that this and similar programs will be of relevance to experienced

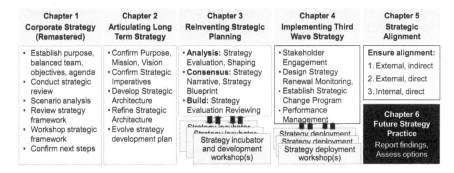

Chapter 1 Corporate Strategy (Remastered)	Chapter 2 Articulating Long Term Strategy	Chapter 3 Reinventing Strategic Planning	Chapter 4 Implementing Third Wave Strategy	Chapter 5 Strategic Alignment
• Establish purpose, balanced team, objectives, agenda • Conduct strategic review • Scenario analysis • Review strategy framework • Workshop strategic framework • Confirm next steps	• Confirm Purpose, Mission, Vision • Confirm Strategic Imperatives • Develop Strategic Architecture • Refine Strategic Architecture • Evolve strategy development plan	• **Analysis:** Strategy Evaluation, Shaping • **Consensus:** Strategy Narrative, Strategy Blueprint • **Build:** Strategy Evaluation Reviewing	• Stakeholder Engagement • Design Strategy Renewal Monitoring, • Establish Strategic Change Program • Performance Management	**Ensure alignment:** 1. External, indirect 2. External, direct 3. Internal, direct
		Strategy incubator and development workshop(s)	Strategy deployment workshop(s)	**Chapter 6 Future Strategy Practice** Report findings, Assess options

Figure 0.1 An overview of chapter structure reflecting the Strategic Management Framework and action plan used in this book

and emerging senior leaders – those who understand fundamental concepts in strategy but are seeking to take their understanding of it to the next level.

> *When applied as a teaching program or consulting methodology, participants are able to work at the same pace and in harmony with internal or external consultants in the development and ownership of their own strategy content.*

In presenting an overview of the book, you will observe from Figure 0.1 that its content follows the same infrastructure deployed in the generic construct of the *Corporate Strategy (Remastered)* I companion book but from a more practical/'doing' perspective. An illustration of the framework used to structure a Third Wave Strategy system appears in Chapter 1 (Figure 1.1) of this book in the form of the Third Wave Strategy framework.

Workshop case study: Third-wave Industries (T-wI), Security Printing and Packaging Division (SPPD)

In our exploration of the topic of business strategy throughout this fieldbook, references will be made to an ongoing case study that is focused on a fictional corporation, albeit one based on a combination of real businesses. The story that unfolds centres on the transformation and renewal of the Security Printing and Packaging Division (SPPD) of parent company Third-wave Industries (T-wI).

Introduction

An overview and description of T-wI and SPPD's current strategic position appears as Case example 0.1. As the story of SPPD unfolds in each chapter it provides an analysis of a corresponding element of the Third Wave Strategy framework. For the purpose of discussion, a representation of the alignment between each chapter and associated element of the framework is presented as Figure 0.1. Our intent is to provide readers with an understanding of the positioning of discussions taking place within each chapter.

Work plan for program of transformation and renewal at T-wI, SPPD

As you will see in our discussion of SPPD, Division Managing Director Jenny Wong and Chief Strategy Officer (CSO) Alicia Manning make several attempts at defining both Long and Short Term Strategy content before a final implementation program can be developed, signed off and commenced. They will be guided by the work plan designed by ex-consultant Alicia Manning and presented as Table 0.1. Although the primary components of the work plan in our journey of discovery are well articulated, we don't follow the strict sequence as set out in the plan. It is unlikely that you will either when you apply the concepts of Third Wave Strategy to practice with your client or directly in your organisation.

The story of transformation and renewal at T-wI, SPPD

The SPPD story, describes how newly appointed Division Managing Director Jenny Wong and her recently appointed CSO Alicia Manning sought to design, develop and then implement a Long Term Strategy. The initial focus of the strategy was the design of a program of organisational transformation and renewal. Their objective in this endeavour was to "turn around SPPD performance while at the same time capitalise on the evolving digital revolution to meet disruption head on". In its implementation their intent was to "transform SPPD into a High Performance Organisation – HPO".

Setting: Now grappling with their survival, a strategic review of SPPD conducted by external consultants presented some hard truths that were difficult to digest. Their findings are presented and discussed in Case example 0.1.

Table 0.1 Development and delivery of a strategy and leadership development program at SPPD

Phase 1: form team, design program	Chapter 1
1 **Build a 'balanced' team**: Confirm purpose and objectives. Learn the concepts of Third Wave Strategy	
2 **Direction setting – confirm**: Purpose of SPPD strategy, objectives, problems to be resolved, desired outcomes and time frames. Explore statements of Purpose, Mission, Vision.	
3 **Conduct situation analysis**: Conduct review and assess context of strategy; explore potential Third Wave Strategy framework Review and assess implications of strategic review	
4 **Conduct scenario analysis**: Evaluate and assess implications	
5 **Conduct**: Facilitate strategy development and incubator mini-workshop(s) with the leadership team	
6 **Confirm next steps**: Build support, obtain commitment	

Table 0.1 (Continued)

Phase 2: establish details of the Long Term Strategy	Chapter 2

1 **Develop, articulate and confirm**: Purpose, Mission, Vision/Long Term Strategy
2 **Establish Strategic Imperatives**
3 **Build preliminary Strategic Architecture**
4 **Review and revise**: Long Term Strategy, confirm next steps
5 **Rework, frame and reframe**: Strategic Architecture
6 **Evolve strategy development plan**

Phase 3: Strategy Evaluation	Chapter 3

1 **Conduct analysis**: Strategy Evaluation, Shaping and incubator workshop(s)
2 **Form consensus**: Final Strategic Architecture, Strategy Narrative, draft Strategy Blueprint, Strategy Evaluation, Reviewing program
3 **Establish support network**: Internal change management agency, 'Community of Strategy Practice' (COSP), foundation of formal organisation learning facility
4 **Design**: Strategy Evaluation, Reviewing network and infrastructure
5 **Confirm next steps**: Follow Program of Continual Strategy Renewal

Phase 4: Strategy Implementation	Chapter 4

Work plan follows worksheets built into content contained in Chapters 4, 5 and 6. Primary objective:
Implement Program of Continual Strategy Renewal:

- Stakeholder Engagement,
- Strategy Renewal Monitoring,
- Strategic Change Program,
- Performance measurement, management. monitoring and reporting mechanism

Phase 5: establish alignment monitoring capability	Chapter 5

Identify and establish monitoring capability for alignment touch points

Phase 6: report findings, assess future options	Chapter 6

Case example 0.1: T-wI: a strategic overview

T-wI was formed in the mid-1970s, following the merger of two family-owned printing and packaging companies. Since that time, T-wI has grown exponentially and is now a listed (London Stock Exchange) corporation with international representation. The company employs 32,000 people worldwide and records annual sales of $3.1 billion. T-wI's core business remains printing and packaging; however, as a result of an acquisition in the mid-1990s, it now has a strong and independent division it refers to as the Security Printing and Packaging Division (SPPD).

SPPD

SPPD is the smallest division at T-wI. As a commodity-based packaging giant, it provides specialist, security-focused printing; packaging and speciality solutions; and advice. Products include authentication and security features for banknotes, passports, certificates, medical and defence packaging. Technologies deployed include holograms, embedded detection devices, barcodes, radio frequency identification (RFID tags) – emitters and receivers, satellite-based Global Positioning System tracking, remote closed-circuit television monitoring, security consulting and advice and a range of other lower volume but related products.

SPPD operating performance

SPPD supplies a range of nonspecific markets and enjoys a history of solid growth; current performance, however, is less than impressive. Its prospects should be significant in an environment of emergent digital technology. T-wI directors, however, are not convinced that it is sufficiently well positioned to optimise its potential from these powerful but seemingly elusive technologies. Acting in sympathy with the board's opinion, T-wI Chief Executive Officer (CEO) Gene Arrowsmith recently announced that he had appointed external consultants to conduct a strategic review of SPPD. Knowing it faced considerable problems, he also promoted Chief Operating Officer Jenny Wong to the leadership position of Managing Director. Jenny in turn moved to appoint a CSO whose priority would be to assist with the transformation of the business once the consultant's report was received.

Reframing strategy practice at T-wI, SPPD

All hopes of a turnaround at T-wI were now heavily placed on Jenny's shoulders and her newly appointed CSO Alicia Manning. Widely respected across the company for their competence in management and leadership, Jenny and Alicia were very keen to learn about and then apply the systems-based strategy concepts that are the very essence of Third Wave Strategy. Alicia read about them when she was a senior employee of the consulting firm that conducted the strategic review of SPPD. She didn't have a lot of experience in its implementation, though.

As the first CSO to be appointed to the role at T-wI, Alicia saw her appointment as a stepping stone to other senior leadership roles in T-wI and accepted the challenge gladly. She was a little reserved at first. She felt that she still had a lot more work to do to transform the way that the high-tech security printing and packaging industry, in particular, operated. She was, however, comforted by the knowledge that she could exert more influence from her corporate position while also evolving her ideas at a practical level. Her first assignment was quite clear and indeed, quite urgent: "To work with the newly appointed Managing Director of T-wI, SPPD Jenny Wong and to work with the leadership team to transform its poor performance into that of a High Performance Organisation – HPO".

Overview: T-wI, SPPD

In their first meeting since their respective appointments, Alicia and Jenny discussed the strategic challenges facing SPPD. The starting point didn't look good:

- Sales had flatlined at an annual revenue of approximately $1.2 billion for the last three years.
- Employee satisfaction ratings had sunk to 83% satisfied, the lowest level since records commenced five years ago.
- Return on investment declined by 3% last year, and plans for new investment, along with its recently released five-year strategic plan, weren't impressing many people, especially T-wI CEO Gene Arrowsmith and the board of directors.
- Customer ratings were stable but not rising, and SPPD was feeling the heat from environmental activists who were applying pressure on the T-wI Corporation to reduce or eliminate the use of plastics in their products.

SPPD has an operational and trading presence in North America, Europe, Australasia and the Middle East. It has long harboured the idea of expansion of sales representation at least into Asia, South America, Russia and the Baltic States.

The tone of the conversation between Jenny and Alicia was far from positive. Jenny described the division as a business with a lot of potential but also one in need of immediate rectification. Her observations were echoed in the report compiled by the external consultants that Alicia had had a hand in writing. A summary follows:

> "We describe SPPD's core business as underachieving but stable and mature. Given its current performance trajectory, its future faces a high level of uncertainty. Its brand recognition, history and breadth of market presence appear to offer only a comparative (as opposed to

a competitive) advantage. SPPD's high-volume, low-margin sales are derived from basic security features that are embedded in its printing and packaging solutions. Examples include medical, defence and high-value (alcohol and cigarettes) consumable items. Higher margin, but lower volume sales are realised from its growing specialty security features and specialist consulting advice. Increasingly, SPPD is facing threats of loss of market share to independent, agile and specialist start-ups.

Against this negativity, however, many opportunities for a turnaround have been identified with a few impactful short term gains available quite quickly. The jewel in the crown is SPPD's new product design and development function. It is one of the few areas to have maintained a positive attitude towards the future. At the same time, it benefits from access to its state-of-the-art equipment and capabilities.

A transformation of SPPD's current operations in its entirety is essential. Questions to be considered include what SPPD should transform to, how the transformation should be affected and what the expected outcomes should be. The answers require a rethinking of current strategy, a reinvigoration of the leadership team and staff and an investment in the 'right' resource base to justify future investment. All improvements must be made with a view to improving profitability, regenerating SPPD's customer satisfaction and market presence, ramping up its points of differentiation and developing aggressive strategy when describing its long term outlook and the necessary actions to be taken to guarantee its survival.

Operating performance did not compare well against benchmarks with similar organisations in the industry. Considerable opportunities for improvement in bottom-line performance were identified. These could be delivered through a reduction of overhead and associated expenses. Solutions proposed include the introduction of aggressive cost-reduction initiatives. These could be achieved through a pruning of excessive staff; the deletion of many minor products, services and brands; and the outsourcing of many essential but 'non-strategic' assets and functions.

Clarification of opportunities for the realisation of future top-line growth required further development. As a potentially high tech, environmentally aware company, options included concepts that extended beyond the more traditional bottom-line, cost reduction solutions mentioned earlier. Our review identified some major new product opportunities and, indeed, industry-breaking ideas that could prove to be very profitable for the business."

Highly experienced in cost reduction and business process redesign activities, Jenny sought to obtain further, more personalised, information about the current status of SPPD. She charged Alicia with the task of extending the initial strategic review to obtain greater detail and clarity. Details of the relevant steps Alicia applied to the conduct of the strategic review are described Table 0.1: Development and delivery of a strategy and leadership development program at SPPD.

Specific characteristics of the current operating environment that Alicia uncovered as part of the consultant's review and beyond are described as follows:

1   SPPD supplies a limited range of specialist security-focused printing and packaging products that are predominantly plastics based. New eco-friendly materials are becoming more readily available.
2   SPPD has approximately a 60% share of the markets in which it has a presence. It employs 11,000 people worldwide.
3   Under the previous SPPD Division managing director, the consultants reported the following organisational profile:

    •   **Aspirations:** Low. Basking in past glories, the desire to reinvigorate and take on new challenges is minimal. Even so, the members of the executive team are loyal, proud and committed to the business. They appeared, however, to lack passion, energy and vision. Most importantly, they seemed not to share any common sense of purpose, making leadership quite difficult, with each senior executive prone to 'doing their own thing'.
    •   **Culture:** Bureaucratic with a strong orientation towards 'traditional' values and ways of doing things, therefore little recent uptake of innovations in product or process.
    •   **Environment:** Lacks an awareness of society's increasingly negative view of a reliance on plastics. SPPD uses these extensively in its traditional, less security-focused commodity products, such as single-use medical containers, consumer product wraps, general product and container packaging and cosmetics labels and packaging.
    •   **Executive team:** Conservative. While only a few 'energised' senior executives could be found, the clear standout was previous Divisional Director of Operations Jenny Wong (now Managing Director).
    •   **Management capability:** Average. A lack of enthusiasm and weak leadership has been the primary cause of inadequate levels of, and needed improvements in, performance.

- **Operating performance:** Below average. SPPD faces increasing pressure on its static sales, market share and profitability.
- **Performance measurement:** Adequate. The firm's performance measurement, management, monitoring and reporting systems are slow, difficult to use and limited in data quality.
- **Customer perspective:** Moderate. Great design competency, well-respected brand name, but an average reputation for service and reliability.
- **Competitiveness:** Low. Increasing emergence of new competitors and existing smaller operators that benefit from lower costs and faster responses to customer needs.
- **Potential:** T-wI, SPPD has forgotten how to act like a 'living' company. It has suffered a loss of purpose and lacks skills in areas that would otherwise represent its essential 'core competences'. In a more positive context, SPPD still has a positive reputation and a strong market presence, and it can benefit from its dominant market share. As the only international supplier in the industry, it enjoys the privilege of very loyal and large corporate customers. They are, however, visibly disheartened with the declining levels of interest in them and a lack of flexibility in costs. They are still content with product quality but warn that SPPD should 'watch this space' on future loyalty.

Fundamental component of Third Wave Strategy: sponsive strategic change

Fundamental to the conduct of our strategic analysis at T-wI is the backdrop of sponsive strategic change, a concept discussed at length in the companion to this book, *Corporate Strategy (Remastered) I*. As explained in that book, an organisation must be equally prepared to adapt to change as much as it is to invent it. It is recommended, therefore, that practitioners embrace a perspective of strategic thinking that introduces the idea of recognising and exploiting the notions of both adaptation and invention:

- Adaptation is concerned with the management of responses to anticipated and unanticipated change.
- Invention is concerned with the deliberate design and creation of one or multiple new futures that in many cases will be created through deliberately disruptive means.

We refer to the process of adaptation as a reactive or proactive **response** *to change we can see or expect. Equally, we propose the use of the term* **prosponse** *as an appropriate reference to reactive or proactive invented* *change that points us towards an envisaged future of what we "can't see but could be".*

In the absence of a clear appreciation of the relationship between *re* and *pro*sponse, each are explained as follows:

1 **Response:** Adaptive strategic change adopted by an organisation that is provoked into an action that is the outcome of an expected or unexpected external or internal stimulus that occurs beyond our control, thereby initiating programs of survival.
2 **Prosponse:** An invented strategic change within our control that is evoked as a result of a deliberate intent to positively challenge or disrupt an organisation's future strategic trajectory, thereby initiating programs of thrival.

In this context sponse is defined as

> *a knowledge-driven change in direction that is provoked or evoked as an outcome from a change in the organisation's circumstances or as a result of the identification of new opportunity that has become apparent within a system's internal and/or external environment.*

To add clarity, four different perspectives of sponsive strategic change are illustrated in the matrix shown in Figure 0.2. Here you will observe an interpretation and description of the environment within which various companies in the personal transport industry can be recognised for their states of 'sponsiveness' with regard to degrees of reactive and proactive behaviours.

There's no doubt that the idea of buying a car, paying for insurance and maintenance and then watching it depreciate to half its value is nowhere as 'worth it' as it used to be. The attraction of such a liberty is reducing considerably with the continual increase in road congestion and smog. No wonder companies such as Apple, Dyson and Google sought to invest in new operating designs and forms of ownership in the mid- to late 2010s. Out of the highest profile start-ups in this space, only Tesla and Alphabet's Waymo are gaining traction. Traditional car companies, however, are fighting back, each with their own approaches to ownership, energy choices and autonomous control mechanisms. No matter what their choice is, there is only one thing that is certain; that is, all industry participants face extreme levels of disruption. We reflect the current state of preparedness for change in each of the quadrants of the sponse matrix illustrated in Figure 0.2. They are discussed as follows:

Quadrant 1, Inertia: Personal transport taxi services in this quadrant commenced with the horse and buggy, a service that was immediately adopted by car owners once automobiles became reliable enough to do so. Other than automated booking and communications, little changed over the years. That was until web-enabled technologies and alternative

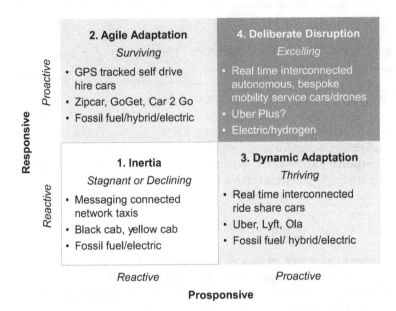

Figure 0.2 Matrix of sponsive strategic change

energy choices provided an incentive to experiment with more inventive solutions.

Quadrant 2, Agile Adapters: Self-drive hire cars were an early adaptive invention. Seeking to take the cost burden of car ownership and energy consumption out of the driver's investment equation, self-drive cars offer similar convenience to ownership. Instead of home-based garages, users can reach their cars within moments, at least, in the neighbourhoods where they have a presence. Operating companies include Zipcar, GoGet and Car 2 Go. They enjoy the same utilisation as taxis, but do not need to pay drivers or parking fees, as local government authorities provide the exclusive parking spaces.

Quadrant 3, Dynamic Adapters: Participants in this space include Uber, Ola and Lyft. Each are referred to as ride-hailing companies; they provide an online booking and personal transportation service in much the same format as would a taxi. Although many taxi companies have survived an onslaught from ride-hailing start-ups, they have had to fight to maintain their existence for some time. Operating as a web-enabled, interactive and real-time monitoring system, the ride-hailing companies' solution is considerably more advanced than most taxi services. Uber is, on the whole, winning the battle, although their success has been far from easy. In addition to the traditional taxi road warriors, Uber has led the way;

however, Ola and Lyft continue to fight Uber in their capacity as commodity price takers rather than price setters.

As the leader in this form of taxi service delivery, Uber has extended its service by leveraging its core competences in technology and customer service into other areas. These include a restaurant delivery service and a 'micro-mobility' system in some countries where it hires out electric bikes and scooters.

Quadrant 4, Deliberate Disruption: Now entering the realm of a Deliberate Disruptor, Uber sees and describes itself as being much more than a ride-hailing business. In a format that could be described as 'Uber Plus' the company sees and describes itself as a full-blown technology company. Its official name is, in fact, Uber Technologies, Inc. According to its website (2019), Uber suggested,

"In addition to helping you get from point A to point B, we're working to bring the future closer with self-driving technology and urban air transport, helping people order food quickly and affordably, removing barriers to healthcare, creating new freight-booking solutions, and helping companies provide a seamless employee travel experience."

Uber Plus won't need to rely on drivers to get people around. As autonomous vehicles, these cars will appear on demand. When there is a reduction in demand, they will go and park in a specific compact location. The type of vehicle will be tailored to individual needs. A business vehicle could include mobile communication capabilities to facilitate group meetings – literally 'on the go'. Family vehicles could include a range of entertainment features. Regular daily commutes to work could include basic, low-cost vehicles that can fit two to six people depending on user demand.

1 Concept of Corporate Strategy (Remastered)

Chapter overview

The focus of our attention in our remastering of strategy is the development of the concept of Third Wave Strategy. Its practice can be distilled down to two key elements. First is its structuring in the form of a systemic, dynamic and fully integrated Strategic Management Framework. Second are the human behavioural aspects of strategy. They consist of cognition and organisational change, Stakeholder Engagement and the conduct of strategy at the standard of a profession.

In explaining our translation of the concept of Third Wave Strategy into practice, a demonstration of its application can be observed through the lens of the Security Printing and Packaging Division (SPPD) of the fictional Third-wave Industries (T-wI) Corporation. SPPD is in trouble; its only way out is to embark on a strategically focused program of organisational transformation and renewal. We introduce in this chapter the fundamental components of the Third Wave Strategy framework and its contribution to the realisation of transformational change. In our explanation of the human behavioural elements of Third Wave Strategy, real cases studies are also used to explain concepts that will inform and influence a leadership team's ability to reframe and thereby bring about lasting and sustainable change.

Learning insights

The key component of introducing and mastering organisational change is an understanding of what needs to change, why it needs to change and, most of all, how to change it. None of this understanding will make any difference, however, unless practitioners can understand what it is that they need to change to.

SPPD has a problem. Newly appointed Division Managing Director Jenny Wong and her cohort CSO Alicia Manning know that SPPD needs to change, and quickly. To institute and lead the transformation required, they must work with and through an executive team that has not experienced change for some time. Jenny and Alicia start their transformation journey, therefore, at a very low level. Through the facilitation of a scenario analysis, they demonstrate how the leadership team can imagine, explore and agree upon a new perspective of a future SPPD and their common understanding of what they must change to.

Once that picture is established, they are introduced to a big picture view of Third Wave Strategy practices that will represent the learning and journey of change upon which they are about to embark. Your learning includes an explanation of the way that scenario analysis works; how to conduct a strategic review; how the team can reframe and think 'differently'; how the construct, components and working of the fully integrated Third Wave Strategy framework can help them to make it all happen; and a how capacity for reframing will enable them to make the transformation successful, or not.

Work plan phase 1: establish details of Long Term Strategy

We base our discussion on the content depicted in the first phase of the project work plan presented as Table 1.1. This is not a strictly structured program. As in real life, its application to practice follows a chaotic rather than fully predictable journey.

Table 1.1 Development and delivery of a strategy and leadership development program at SPPD: Phase I

Phase 1: form team, design program	Chapter 1

1. **Build a 'balanced' team:** Confirm purpose and objectives. Learn concepts of Third Wave Strategy
2. **Direction setting – confirm:** Purpose of SPPD strategy, objectives, problems to be resolved, desired outcomes, time frames. Explore statements of Purpose, Mission, Vision.
3. **Conduct situation analysis:** Conduct review and assess context of strategy, explore potential Third Wave Strategy framework, review and assess implications of strategic review
4. **Conduct scenario analysis:** Evaluate and assess implications
5. **Conduct:** Facilitate strategy development and incubator mini-workshop(s) with the leadership team
6. **Confirm next steps:** Build support, obtain commitment

Introduction: Concept of Corporate Strategy (Remastered)

As the instrument providing structure to strategy and the structure of this book, the story commences with an analysis of the primary vehicle that enabled us to design the remastering of strategy; the Third Wave Strategy framework as illustrated in Figure 1.1.

This framework is representative of a dynamic, open system which provides guidelines, structure and boundaries to Third Wave Strategy practice. The purpose of the framework, it is stressed, is to complement and facilitate human interaction, individual and team behaviour and the complexity of cognitive strategy practice but not to replace it. Supplementary to our discussion about

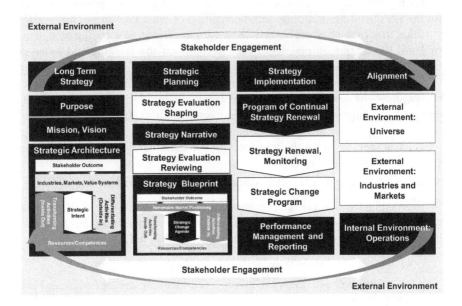

Figure 1.1 Third Wave Strategy framework

the framework, therefore, we also address in this chapter the human and behavioural-oriented topics of cognition and organisational change, Stakeholder Engagement and professional strategy practice. The combination is demonstrated in Figure 1.2.

With these topics in mind, our discussion commences with an introduction to the subject of our case study, T-wI, SPPD. Key to this introduction is an appreciation of the company and its future, enunciated via an assessment of a strategic review (Case example 0.1), the conduct of a scenario analysis and an assessment of the implications.

Transforming T-wI, SPPD: a need to reframe, transform and renew

As suggested in our introduction to the SPPD story in Case example 0.1, newly appointed Division Managing Director Jenny Wong and her recently appointed CSO Alicia Manning have been given the task of addressing the issues identified by specialist consultants who had recently conducted a strategic review of the business. Their findings can be summarised as follows:

> *A transformation of SPPD's current operations in its entirety is essential. To do this, a rethinking of current strategy, a reinvigoration of the leadership team and staff and an investment in the 'right' resource base must be instigated immediately.*

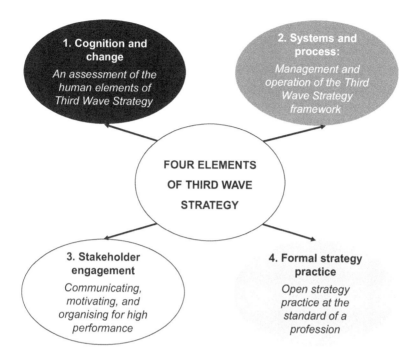

Figure 1.2 Components of Third Wave Strategy

Fundamental to this transformation the consultants identified was the need "to improve profitability, regenerate customer satisfaction and market presence, ramp up points of differentiation and develop an aggressive strategy describing SPPD's long term outlook and the actions that should be taken to guarantee its survival". It was no small task. As a seasoned strategy consultant, however, SPPD CSO Alicia Manning was delighted to take the lead in the proposed T-wI, SPPD transformation journey that awaited her and her colleagues. In her preparation for the journey, Alicia was keen to inform the leadership team of exactly what was in store, what needed to be done and by when. She referred her team, therefore, to the illustrative work plan that she had developed especially for that purpose. It appears as Figure 0.1 and in more detail in Case example 0.1 of this book.

Planning the transformation journey at SPPD

Once SPPD Division Managing Director Jenny Wong signed off on the work plan (Table 0.1), she and Alicia wasted no time in getting started on their transformation journey. In the early stages, Alicia and Jenny were the only members of the project team. Resisting an urge to follow her instincts by diving straight into a savage restructuring and cost-reduction program, Jenny acknowledged that their first task should be to get a handle on exactly what the dimensions of the restructuring program would be and what its objectives were.

Fundamental to the challenge they faced was the fact that SPPD was wallowing in a non-sponsive state of Inertia as depicted in Figure 0.1. Both Jenny and Alicia agreed the first imperative they faced lay in stabilising and reinvigorating SPPD's leadership. Not only did the leadership team and staff need be convinced of the need for change, they also needed to accept that drastic measures were required to deliver that change. To do this, they realised they would need all employees to reframe and literally reconceptualise their current perspective of the business. Their immediate need, Jenny observed, was to find a way to evolve a greater sense of purpose and urgency, as well as a higher level of motivation. Most of all, they needed to deliver a significantly higher level of operating performance if they were to simply survive.

To get their journey underway, their primary objective was to lay the foundation for the development and ownership of a redefined SPPD-specific strategy. In this sense, they recognised that

> *it wasn't the strategy document that was going to make the difference. Rather, it was what was contained in it and that everyone owned it. That would be achieved by an articulation, understanding and acceptance of the actions they would need to take in order to relieve SPPD of its state of inertia and set it on a more prosperous and rewarding trajectory of Hyper – High Performance permanently.*

Consistent with the recommendation made by Corporate High Performance Specialist deWaal (2010), they identified their first task as being to

> *set a vision that excites, challenges and creates clarity; evokes a common sense of purpose, an understanding of where it wants to go and how to get there – in other words, its strategy.*

SPPD's leadership team had no current appreciation of any of the concepts of good strategy, never mind the establishment of a Hyper – HPO. The need to know, however, provided fertile ground for Alicia and Jenny to engage with them in open dialogue as they sought to address SPPD's current dilemma. It was a need to reframe, to think differently and to take appropriate action.

Reframing through social engagement: application of scenario analysis

In order to develop a vision that excites a common sense of purpose and the foundation of a Long Term Strategy, Alicia chose to start the program with the conduct of a scenario analysis. This is an analytical tool that is included in the second element of the Third Wave Strategy framework (Figure 1.1): Strategy Evaluation, Shaping (presented in detail in Chapter 3). Alicia had gained some experience in the use of this tool in her previous consulting role. Her reasoning in choosing it now was threefold. First, she was comfortable that it would satisfy the need to develop an understanding of SPPD's current position. Second, she saw it as a tool that would help her colleagues understand what their organisation might look like in a world some 20 to 50 years into the future. Third, and most importantly,

> *Alicia was keen to use scenario analysis as a tool to engage senior leaders in open dialogue.*

Even though she recognised scenarios were only a representation of an imagined future, she knew they would provide a platform upon which

- a common language could be normalised, and, just as importantly,
- a reframing and broad-based Stakeholder Engagement program could be formed.

These, she hoped, would encourage the 'right' discussions to take place and thereby allow alternative points of view to be developed, team comradery built, decisions made and an approach to transformation envisaged and, ideally, agreed.

Use of scenario analysis in practice

As pioneers in the field of scenario planning, Shell provides insight into the use and application of scenario analysis. On their website, Shell note that it is important that the insight generated is representative of a distinctly plausible 'being'. Good scenarios, they suggest, are ones that explore the possible, not just the probable. They are the scenarios that provide a relevant challenge to conventional wisdom. Insight delivered helps them prepare for the major challenges ahead. Here is the real value though, as according to Shell:

> *Good scenarios provide a useful context for debate that leads to better policy and strategy, and a shared understanding of, and commitment to action.*

We do not recommend, therefore, the use of scenarios to attempt to predict a specific outcome in the future. Rather, scenarios are best used to capture the power of a 'commonly shared and owned story of the future' (de Geus, 1988). This has been found to be an extremely useful way to engage and unite a team around a common sense of purpose and direction.

Application of scenario analysis to SPPD

Alicia and Jenny prepared to conduct the scenario analysis in SPPD with input from a number of sources. These included the external consultant's report (Case example 0.1) and the views, concerns and observations from the individual members of the leadership team and other stakeholders and members of the T-wI corporate office. A first-hand appreciation of the issues she had gleaned from her involvement with the consultant's report were confirmed from a follow-up, deep-dive strategic review she conducted on her own. Included in Case example 1.1 is an overview of the steps that Alicia followed to conduct a strategic review.

Case example 1.1: Strategy Evaluation, Reviewing: conducting a strategic review

1   **Iterative strategy review cycle:** Ongoing discussions and interviews with the CEO, senior leaders, directors and other stakeholders

    i   **Confirm the purpose of SPPD strategy:** Why do we need a strategy? What are desired outcomes? Confirm value of strategy and ascertain strength of existing strategy and firm's capability in strategy practice

    ii   Confirm expectations from strategy, articulate expected outcomes

    iii **Agree approach to strategy review and process:**

        a   **Confirm project plan**

        b   **Assess context:** Strategic Imperative? New leader? Acquisition/new business, quadrant in sponse matrix

        c   **Confirm objectives:** How do we want to use findings, and who will we communicate with?

2   **Conduct situation analysis**: Review

    i   Comparative studies, external consultant reports

    ii   Environmental scanning – political, industrial, economic, social, technological or environmental (PESTE) analysis, scenario analysis

    iii Review other background documents

    iv   Conduct interviews with relevant personnel, complete site tours, engage others in project

3   **Diagnose**

    i   Collect facts about current strategy, strategy process, structure, content, alignment and comprehensiveness (the Strategic Management Framework is a useful guide)

    ii Evaluate industry, organisational, international context and their impact on strategy

    iii Tease out real strategic issues to be addressed

    iv Use Strategic Architecture, Integrated Value System, strategic equilibrium, sponse matrix, Strategy Blueprint, risk monitoring, other analytical tools and worksheets where appropriate

4 **Assess broader picture:** Interview more executives, managers and employees

    i Test hypothesis and assumptions and basis for issue resolution

    ii Appraise strength and understanding of underlying policies

    iii Tease out real strategic issues facing the firm

    vi Assess real sources of power and individual judgement and insight

    v Identify, compare and confirm basis and validity of strategic imperatives

    vi Assess capacity to implement

5 **Conclude**

    i Build preliminary Strategic Architecture

    ii Articulate initial observations and findings, draw conclusions

6 **Test:** Interviews, test for validity, detailed analysis, modelling, simulation

7 **Prepare draft report/presentation:** Summarise findings in report format as a draft

8 **Review findings:** Discuss with CEO/responsible person/people, test for validity, complete documentation and get sign off

9 **Communicate:** Provide individual feedback where required and present to leadership team

Armed with her now detailed understanding of the strategic issues facing SPPD, Alicia felt quite comfortable that she really understood their current position. She also felt confident now to work with Jenny in the development of a scenario analysis for the division as the first step in their journey towards transformation. Alicia reviewed a broad range of methods of scenario analysis to get to the approach described here. Examples include those provided by Georgantzas and Acar (1995), Godet and Roubelat (1985), and Schwartz and Ogilvy (1998).

The generic methodology she applied was as follows:

Step 1: understand the big picture: Identify the primary issues of concern in the external environment

Step 2: assess areas of internal conflict: These are the pressing areas of concern that need to be addressed and resolved

Step 3: identify the main focal issue or question to be addressed

Step 4: identify two 'critical' areas of uncertainty and list them by priority: These are the areas where the greatest causes of uncertainty may lie

Step 5: flesh out the uncertainties: Develop plausible scenarios of the future

Step 6: assess implications: Draw conclusions and make recommendations

Each of these steps are discussed as follows:

Step 1: understand the big picture: identify the primary issues of concern in the external environment

The purpose of this preliminary step is to provide direction and insight to the team's future-focused thinking. In the identification of topics to review, it is proposed that the technique of environmental scanning is applied at each of the two levels of external environmental influence that are identified and listed as follows:

Level 1: Outside In, external indirect: Universally focused environmental scanning

Level 2: Outside In, external, direct: Industry- and market-level analysis

An analysis of issues of relevance to each at SPPD follows.

Level 1: Outside In, external indirect: universally focused environmental scanning

A common tool deployed for the purpose of environmental scanning at Level 1 is that of an analysis of the political, economic, social, technological and ecological (PESTE) analysis. PESTE analysis is used to identify areas of greatest uncertainty in the external environment. This insight is used to obtain an appreciation of how and by how much these factors will impact company performance in future years. As a contributor to scenario analysis, PESTE analysis provides insight into the strategy practitioner's understanding of such issues as economic growth or decline, technological and social trends, emerging political realities and impact of globalisation.

Alicia chose to include a PESTE analysis in the scenario analysis exercise being conducted at SPPD. The results are presented in Case example 1.2.

Case example 1.2: PESTE analysis of relevance to T-wI, SPPD scenario analysis

Instructions: Identify up to two to three areas of greatest uncertainty that could impact your world and your industry in the next 10–15 years.

Response

Political issues:

- Significantly raised interest in increasing the use of 'smart' packaging delivering, better product 'information', traceability, security features, 'tamper-proof' solutions and the impact of the product on the environment.
- Significant increase in pressure from the government to tighten security 'across the board' following cyberattacks and hacking via standard Internet connections.

Economic issues:

- Global increase in oil price that adversely influences the core cost of plastics.
- Increases in fluctuation in currency exchange rates whose primary impact is also on cost.
- Ongoing development of 'fair' trade agreements as opposed to 'free' trade agreements, resulting in better access to international markets but the reintroduction of tariffs and measures of protection in many countries.

Social issues:

- Increase in demand to provide greater 'disclosure' (product information) to consumers.
- Rising demand for greater privacy protection impacting methods of data collection, physical tracking of goods and their owners and the use of surveillance cameras and other similar equipment.

Technological issues:

- Transmogrification of product definitions – e.g. from barcode security tags to integrated, web enabled security systems.
- Significant increase in use of e-commerce with 'smart packaging' used as a delivery mechanism.

- Strong trend towards high-tech solutions that require greater engagement of suppliers and customers consistent with the emergence of the eco-friendly 'circular' economy. According to the WRAP website, "a circular economy is an alternative to a traditional linear economy (make, use, dispose) in which we keep resources in use for as long as possible, extract the maximum value from them whilst in use, then recover and regenerate products and materials at the end of each service life".
- Rapid advances in use of smart chips, radio frequency identification and bio metrics.

Ecological issues:

- Global trends to ban the use of plastics-based packaging altogether.
- Rising trend away from 'showy', high-value materialistic products that provide minimal functionality.
- Global trend against smoking and thereby cigarette packaging an emerging high-value, high-risk security threat.

Volatility, uncertainty, complexity and ambiguity (VUCA)

The notion of VUCA was added to this list because it is an emerging phenomenon that if nothing else will help to narrow the list of the areas of greatest concern when deciding topics for inclusion in the matrix of greatest uncertainty. When taken into consideration following the PESTE analysis completed earlier, it became quite apparent to the SPPD leadership that the social change that has been and will continue to be brought about by emerging technology was *complex* because of its technological and social interactivity. It was also *ambiguous* because although there was significant evidence to allow an assessment of technology to take place, in reality, this was only a precursor to what is to come. Given the *complexity* of the technological developments underway, it is not clear just how the emerging technology will impact the future of business and the future of society. The speed of the rate and enormity of change when it arrives and the speed of development of things impacting future technology combine to deliver an environment of extreme *uncertainty*. Above all else, each of the foregoing elements of VUCA combine to create a large amount of disruption to the global economy.

Level 2: Outside In, external, direct environment: industry- and market-level analysis

At Level 2, Alicia relied on available industry data, technology journals, competitor analysis and competitive intelligence data that had been conducted on a regular basis over the years. She also relied on content included in the results of the strategic reviews that were of relevance to this level of analysis following her involvement in SPPD as a consultant and as an executive. In order to make this an ongoing and live source of data, she appointed an additional resource to her strategy department and assigned them the task of establishing a commercial intelligence system as a separate section of the Tw-I SPPD intranet. This system would have previously been known as a competitive intelligence system. The notion of competitiveness is so vague now it is recommended that much broader sources of data are sought than those of market- and competitor-specific knowledge alone.

> **Step 2: assess areas of internal conflict:** identify the pressing areas of concern that need to be addressed and resolved

In addition to the two levels of Outside In, external environmental analysis an Inside Out, internally focused level of analysis is also explored and discussed next.

Level 3: Inside Out, internal environment: resource and core competence analysis

At Level 3, Alicia was content to incorporate the results of the strategic reviews and the views of a range of stakeholders she had subsequently gathered for analysis. Her specific purpose was to form an opinion as to the identification of 'critical' matters of internal conflict around which the scenario analysis should be conducted. These observations are listed as follows:

- SPPD's core business was declining in both momentum and competitiveness.
- Core business offered limited growth prospects; however, its emerging business offered significant potential to increase profitability, as well as desirable social outcomes.
- Future growth would, however, require an immediate and significant investment in technology and an awareness of the extent and nature of new technology yet to be made available.
- Significant organisational transformation was required if SPPD is to successfully raise its revenues from its emerging businesses.

- A change in attitude and morale was required at the most senior levels of the business if it was to both survive and thrive.

SPPD was once widely recognised as an industry shaper that deployed proprietary technology to deliver high performance results. Two years ago, however, the incumbent managing director introduced changes that led to a re-emphasis on what he called 'core' business. This change followed the release of a cost analysis that showed

- 'high-tech' products were far less profitable than thought,
- capital investment in high-tech solutions was leading SPPD deeper into the 'mire', and
- long term profitability would be boosted by a refocus on simpler, higher volume products.

A salvation for SPPD could be found in the fact that it had retained many of its technical skills and investments in innovation, research and development over the years. When it came down to the wire though, it became apparent that SPPD lacked a commitment to the commercialisation of its 'high-tech' solutions, even though it had the physical capability to do so. So how has the business survived? The determining factors influencing SPPD's customers to buy from them include

- a traditional but good quality product,
- a reasonable price with local supply (although becoming less of an advantage),
- predictable levels of service delivery (stick with the devil you know), and
- access to technical advice and expertise that is received free of charge.

Step 3: identify the main focal issue or question to be addressed:
If there was one thing that the SPPD leadership team had come to understand and accept it was the fact that a great deal of change was required to be made in a very short period of time. What they didn't know was what the change would entail and what they wanted to change to. The main question forming the basis for the scenario analysis became quite obvious, therefore:

What will SPPD look like if it is to prosper, grow and excel up to and beyond the year 2040?

Step 4: identify two 'critical' areas of uncertainty and list by priority:
these are the areas where the greatest causes of uncertainty may lie
As an outcome from the foregoing analysis, and in seeking to provide a framework to address the key question identified earlier, two issues were identified as those presenting the greatest areas of uncertainty:

1   **Horizontal axis:** Uptake in the use of technology (especially 'smart print-ing and packaging') in two areas:

   i   **Operational:** Improve social responsibility, operating efficiency and effectiveness

   ii   **Strategic:** Apply advanced technology, such as artificial intelligence and 'smart packaging', to deliver stakeholder satisfaction, product information, security and tamper-proof solutions to consumers

2   **Vertical axis:** Global pressure to embrace cost-effective, advanced mate-rials capable of capturing and emitting electronic data, as well as socially responsible operations, products and services.

The initial axis of uncertainty that evolved out of that discussion is illustrated in Figure 1.3.

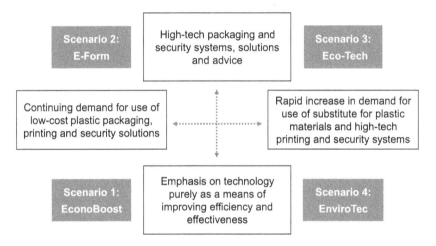

Figure 1.3 Foundation of SPPD futures scenario quadrant – based on axis of greatest uncertainty

Step 5: flesh out the uncertainties: develop plausible scenarios of the future

Insight into the suite of alternative futures developed as an outcome from the scenario analysis led to a reassessment of SPPD's future in a way that was a pleasant surprise to Alicia and the leadership team. A fuller and even richer view was provided by the final scenario matrix presented here as Figure 1.4.

Step 6: assess implications: draw conclusions and make recommendations

In their assessment of the impact of the scenario analysis to SPPD, it was Jenny's view that the future was highly consistent with that described in the Scenario

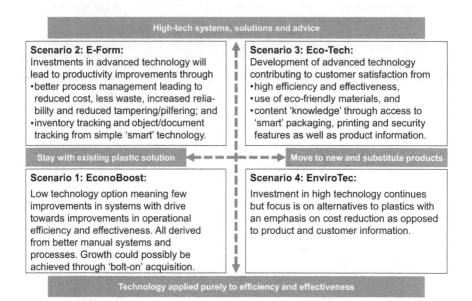

High-tech systems, solutions and advice	
Scenario 2: E-Form: Investments in advanced technology will lead to productivity improvements through • better process management leading to reduced cost, less waste, increased reliability and reduced tampering/pilfering; and • inventory tracking and object/document tracking from simple 'smart' technology.	**Scenario 3: Eco-Tech:** Development of advanced technology contributing to customer satisfaction from • high efficiency and effectiveness, • use of eco-friendly materials, and • content 'knowledge' through access to 'smart' packaging, printing and security features as well as product information.
Stay with existing plastic solution ← − − − − − → **Move to new and substitute products**	
Scenario 1: EconoBoost: Low technology option meaning few improvements in systems with drive towards improvements in operational efficiency and effectiveness. All derived from better manual systems and processes. Growth could possibly be achieved through 'bolt-on' acquisition.	**Scenario 4: EnviroTec:** Investment in high technology continues but focus is on alternatives to plastics with an emphasis on cost reduction as opposed to product and customer information.
Technology applied purely to efficiency and effectiveness	

Figure 1.4 SPPD advanced future scenario matrix

1 EconoBoost. Given the stagnation in growth, lack of motivation and indication of low profitability of high-tech products that prevailed at SPPD, she had readily convinced herself and the leadership team that the insight made sense. The value in the scenario exercise, she now realised, was that she could hold meaningful discussions with the leadership team about SPPD's future. Still caught in the mindset of Ansoff's (1965) planning regime, the whole team agreed with this benefit. Similarly, they were happy to declare a newfound common acceptance of the fact that alternatives do exist. They were all relieved also that they could commence the development of the next 'strategic plan' quite soon, assuming, of course, that the necessary cost-reduction initiatives had delivered their desired effect in time.

Pleased by the leadership team's acceptance for change, but equally stunned by the apparent lack of urgency and inability to look beyond an annualised perspective of strategy, Alicia and Jenny realised that they had a big challenge on their hands. For both, this realisation was quite daunting. How do they turn a stagnant, mature packaging company led by a stagnant, mature leadership team into a Third Wave Strategy Hyper – HPO? One that is ready to take the lead through a capacity to take immediate action to both of the following:

- **Adapt:** Manage a strategy system that is both re and prosponsive when it comes to strategic change

- **Invent:** Establish a strategy that creates new opportunity and new futures altogether

Although the scenario analysis contributed greatly to their appreciation of the opportunity on offer and the task they faced, they were still unsure how to get it underway. They were keen to get to the next step of analysis, which was to understand the application of the Third Wave Strategy framework to their business.

System and process: construct of the Third Wave Strategy framework

Fundamental to the management and operation of our remastered version of strategy (as well as solving Jenny and Alicia's conundrum of identifying where to start) is its structure, which is comfortably encapsulated within the Third Wave Strategy framework (Figure 1.1).

Although the framework should be treated as a system, its natural flow follows a left-to-right sequence. That is, it starts with Purpose, Vision, Mission and ends with an articulation of alignment between strategy and operations. This is the sequence that is followed in our review of the framework now and throughout the book. When in operation, the framework can accommodate an intervention at any place and at any time, as witnessed, for instance, upon the commencement of the review of SPPD. This activity involved the development of a scenario analysis that is straight out of the Strategy Evaluation, Shaping playbook, element 2 of the framework. A brief overview of each of the elements of the framework conducted in sequential order follows.

Element 1: expressions of Purpose, Mission, Vision and Long Term Strategy

In today's corporations, expressions of Purpose, Mission, Vision are articulated as a matter of good governance. Although positive, it would be preferable if they were developed for the purpose of leadership as well. After all,

> *just as we can't be what we can't see, we certainly can't lead anyone into the future if we can't articulate why (purpose), how (mission) or where (vision) we want to go.*

As senior leaders of our illustrative case study (SPPD), Alicia Manning and Jenny Wong would have been only too aware that

> *expressions of a common sense of purpose and direction are critical in defining and confirming a foundation upon which Long Term Strategy can be articulated and high performance leadership can be launched.*

Because the future is hard to envisage, few can imagine or appreciate the opportunity of the ambition that statements of Purpose, Mission, Vision may hold.

Confirming the value of Purpose, Vision, Mission

The task of recognising the value of a statement of purpose is made easier once practitioners understand and appreciate the reason to *do* strategy. It is our opinion that the purpose of strategy is to

> *describe how a firm will realise its organisational purpose through its continual adaptation to foreseen and unforeseen change and the implementation of opportunity driven by innovative inventions introduced as drivers of deliberate and often disruptive change.*

It is purely tradition that dictates that strategically focused planning 'away days' and 'off-sites' start with a reinvention of Purpose, Mission, Vision. In practice, such statements will quite conceivably have been set some time ago. It is precisely for that reason that the content, intent and purpose of Long Term Strategy is rarely seen or discussed. Alarmingly, in the absence of a clear understanding of Purpose, Mission, Vision or a clear articulation of Long Term Strategy, short term plans are susceptible to a whiplash action. What happens next is regrettable:

> *When short term plans are not anchored to a Long Term Strategy and sense of Purpose, Mission, Vision, the foundations will inevitably separate from the core, weaken and eventually collapse.*

As an example of this unfolding saga, look no further than the numerous corporations around the world that continue to reinvent their Long Term Strategy purely by rewriting a short term strategic plan. Rather than attempting to beat the threat from online technology, for example, numerous tradition-bound, brick-to-brick organisations have remained extremely slow to embrace it.

Similarly, in misunderstanding the purpose of strategy, practitioners continue to mistake operational effectiveness with strategic decision making. Here practitioners are prone to confuse the redesign of supply chains, organisational structuring, their application of data analytics and the introduction of automated online payments to tackle the move to online trading as being strategic, not operational, in nature. We believe this to be erroneous. After all,

> *core business didn't change with the arrival of online trading alone. In reality, web-based trading is just another component of the supply chain and another, albeit more efficient, means of reaching the consumer.*

Part of the reason for mistaking operations for strategy is that the analysis used as input to strategic decision making is inadequate. Examples are SWOT analysis, gap analysis and, yes, static, deliberate strategic planning. While useful as 'simple' analytical documents, they are not suited for application to the business environment of today. As illustrated in the Third Wave Strategy framework,

> ***Purpose, Mission, Vision provide a foundation upon which Long Term Strategy can be articulated, Short Term Strategy evolved, implementation designed and articulated and alignment delivered.***

An exploration of an anchor for the framework, that of Long Term Strategy is discussed next.

Long Term Strategy

The essence of Long Term Strategy is captured in the construct of a Strategic Architecture. Prahalad and Hamel (1990) first coined this term; however, they didn't provide a specific construct, which we do. It is described as follows.

Construct of a Strategic Architecture: a tour of discovery

As demonstrated in Figure 1.5, the construct of a Strategic Architecture is designed to provide a visual illustration of an otherwise qualitative description of Long Term Strategy.

At the top of the Strategic Architecture are Stakeholder Outcomes. These are the financial, social and ecological measures of performance that must be met if the organisation is to survive and thrive. These aren't the 'stretch' goals

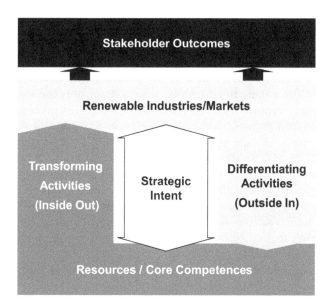

Figure 1.5 An example of a fundamental Strategic Architecture

and targets that are often advocated by pundits from various quarters (Hamel & Prahalad, 1993); they are reserved for Short Term Strategy (Chapter 3).

Other components of the Strategic Architecture contain the Strategic Imperatives that must be met in order for the organisation to realise those Stakeholder Outcomes in the long term. Strategic Imperatives are defined as those things an organisation must have or do if it is to deliver a firm's purpose, desired outcomes and results in the long term.

Content depicted in the Strategic Architecture is organised into two distinct and core orientations:

- **Outside In, customer-focused orientation:** These are descriptions of the universe, economy, industries and markets within which the firm intends to compete. It is also a description of the activities it will embrace in order to differentiate itself from competitors.
- **Inside Out, resource-focused orientation:** These are the collective of tangible and intangible resources and core competencies (strategic assets; Amit and Schoemaker, 1993) of the firm and its transforming activities. The term 'transforming activities' refers to the way an organisation improves its resources or the way it improves the way it improves its resources.

While the current focus for Long Term Strategy at SPPD is a little vague, Alicia's and Jenny's ambition certainly isn't. Both have proposed a decidedly Inside Out approach to strategy through their support of refining or automating much of the SPPD resource base through the enactment of transforming activities. They do recognise at the same time, however, that their understanding and definition of market positioning needs a lot of work also.

Element 2: Strategic planning

The essence of the second element of the framework is its reinvention of the transformation of a static three- to five-year strategic plan and its remastering into a 'Strategy Narrative'. A Strategy Narrative is representative of an ongoing oration rather than a static 'to-do' list. Content includes details of the reasoning, assumptions and expectations behind the Short Term Strategy, as well as intended outcomes. The Strategy Blueprint is derived from the Strategy Narrative. Just as the Strategic Architecture is a representation and construct of a Long Term Strategy, so is the Strategy Blueprint an illustrative construct of Short Term Strategy. Instead of Strategic Imperatives, however, the Strategy Blueprint contains activity-focused Strategic Objectives. These are expressions of the activities that enable the organisation to realise its long term strategic imperatives in the short term.

The content contained in the Strategy Narrative is informed by outcomes from the activities of Strategy Evaluation, Shaping and Strategy Evaluation, Reviewing. It is also the source of data that is summarised and subsequently presented in the construct of a Strategy Blueprint. The purpose of the Strategy

Blueprint is to provide a structure to Short Term Strategy and the associated short term strategic objectives. Each of the elements of Strategy Evaluation are discussed as follows:

Strategy Evaluation, Shaping: This activity can be defined as

the process of formulating the input that will inform Long Term Strategy and content contributing to the makeup of Short Term Strategy.

Key activities include environmental scanning, scenario analysis, market share analysis and other forms of strategic thinking (design thinking, intuition) and analysis.

Strategy Evaluation, Reviewing: This activity can be described as

the act of knowledge accumulation, evaluation and dissemination.

The former two assume a form of adaptation, responding to lessons learned from our own experiences. The latter assumes an act of prosponding – that of knowledge dissemination – to the teaching of lessons taught from the experiences of others inside or outside the company. The act of Strategy Evaluation, Reviewing consists of an assessment of the way in which strategy is managed and the value and relevance of the outcomes from strategy and lessons learned.

Also included and highlighted is the idea of responsive and prosponsive strategy practice in the Strategy Evaluation activity. It is one thing to be concerned with adapting to known and unknown, expected and unexpected eventualities. It is another thing altogether to design and introduce our own ideas of deliberately disruptive futures, especially those based on perceptions of realities of often highly sceptical customers. Apple, Amazon and Google are examples of a growing number of organisations that do this all the time – albeit not always successfully (think of Google Glass as an obvious failure in augmented reality, although commentators would no doubt suggest we haven't seen the last of them yet).

Element 3: Strategy Implementation

Enacted within a Program of Continual Strategy Renewal, this third element of the framework describes the activities that are conducted to implement strategy in the long and the short term. The idea of a Program of Continual Strategy Renewal automatically evokes an aura of dynamic strategy practice; it literally brings the strategy form and function to life. It is an active and mostly mechanistic process; its content is extrapolated from the strategic objectives identified in the Strategy Blueprint. Its purpose is to monitor the ongoing effectiveness and relevance of the assumptions and intuitive judgements that went into strategy formulation. In this context, it enjoys a direct link with the activity of Strategy Evaluation, Reviewing. It is also used to monitor the progress of the Strategic Change Program. This is the control mechanism that leads to the implementation of the programs and projects determined as an outcome from Short Term Strategy.

The overall Program of Continual Strategy Renewal is operated in the form of an embedded performance, measurement, management, monitoring and reporting system. In its operation,

> *any changes in assumptions, projects and programs, along with changes in the sheer reality of business, will cause the strategy practitioner to question and review the effectiveness of (that is re-evaluate) the assumptions and ongoing content included in the Strategy Narrative and associated Strategy Blueprint.*

In all likelihood, the monitoring and reporting mechanism will sit alongside, or integrate with, the regular management reporting mechanism of the company, as demonstrated in Chapter 4.

Element 4: Alignment

As the fourth element of the framework, the purpose of Strategic Alignment is to ensure that strategy remains relevant and responsive to the activities, events and influences that expectedly or unexpectedly occur in the external environment. It is also deployed to ensure that strategy remains relevant to the activities, plots, plans and events that may be created, or accidently occur, within the internal environment.

External environment

As illustrated in Figure 1.1, the workings of the Third Wave Strategy framework takes place within the context of the external environment. As we saw in the SPPD scenario development exercise, we differentiate between Level 1 and Level 2 measures of the external environment. Each represent the world within which the company operates, and strategy is formulated, trialled, adjusted, implemented, reviewed and renewed. The systemic nature of the strategy framework ensures that network connectivity takes place and an integrated system can be made to be truly effective. Although mechanistic in presentation, it must be stressed that the framework depicted in Figure 1.1 is just that – a framework and structure to strategy that supports and informs strategic conversations but doesn't replace them. A discussion about the human influence on strategy and strategic decision making follows.

Cognition and organisational change: an assessment of the human aspects of Third Wave Strategy

This is the second component of Third Wave Strategy, as illustrated in Figure 1.2. It is a topic that, in our view at least, is as important as the mechanistic

Third Wave Strategy framework presented in Figure 1.1. A violin, for example, is an instrument of beauty. Its sound is scratchy and unbearable, however, unless it is played with understanding, commitment, passion, skill and empathy. Similarly, the Third Wave Strategy framework won't lose its rigidity unless it is deployed within a culture that embraces the cognitive and people-oriented attributes of

- an enthusiasm for deep, innovative, original and, when appropriate, intuitive strategic thinking;
- a capacity for decision making based on a combination of hard logic, which is informed by insight, envisaged through foresight and emboldened by the wisdom of hindsight;
- a healthy tolerance for failure as a prime contributor to a broad-based program of organisational learning;
- the enablement of informed dialogue, critical thinking and a community-based approach to decision making and issue/problem resolution;
- a leadership regime that allows for, and actively encourages, a commitment to the trialling of agility (both physical and mental), innovation, exploration and invention; and
- a hunger to drive organisational growth informed by focused strategic intelligence.

Each of these characteristics are immersed in our discussions throughout this chapter and, indeed, this book. Although deemed a critical component of strategy by us, you will no doubt have observed that the deliberate exclusion of the human behavioural aspects of strategy from Ansoff's 1965 'planning regime'; for example, he

unwittingly alienated the function of strategy, condemning it to that of an isolated, ritualistic, annual event rather than a vital, everyday component of the management and control of the business.

With all the will in the world, no spreadsheet, project management tool, competitor-focused strategic plan or market share analysis will mean anything unless all of the 'human' aspects of strategy are deployed to its practice. These practices include and are captured in the framework.

It is our recommendation, therefore, that in order to enable empowerment – at all levels of the organisation – Third Wave Strategy is conducted in an open, cooperative and inclusive environment. The right circumstances for the organisation that you lead now or will lead in the future will be determined by your style of leadership and the organisational culture that you have nurtured or created. It is unlikely that an organisation facing bankruptcy, for example, would be very interested in embracing inclusive open strategy practice. In situations of regeneration, positivity and growth, on the other hand, the circumstances will be more conducive to such an approach.

As an initial observation, practitioners should be aware that in its conduct, there is an imperative for all strategy practitioners to apply a deep and open-minded focus to its practice. This lies in contrast with the all too common, but admittedly more comfortable, close-minded, habit-dominated and mid-brained auto mode that is typically adopted by default in our everyday thinking. While doing that, it is important that all practitioners question the established 'rules' of strategy and, consequently, embrace a program of *learning* and, where necessary, *unlearning*. We take care of the learning element in this book, which by default also alerts you to what you need to unlearn.

Learning and unlearning when engaged in strategy practice? The need to reframe

Survey after survey has shown that there is a very low level of satisfaction with the effectiveness of first and second wave strategy practices (Strategic Management Institute, 2013). Similarly, Bolman and Deal (2017) implied a degree of disappointment with managers' capacity to learn and unlearn:

> *Managers tend to live in psychic prisons; unable to look at old problems in a new light and attack old problems with different and powerful tools – they cannot think differently.*

The solution they suggest is to reframe. When reframing, they invite managers to break down ingrained images (mental models) of the past and instead adopt a process of 'rapid cognition'. This requires them to adopt an inherent, but often hidden, capacity to think, behave, act and react in quick order. An ability to reframe, they observe, will allow them to

> *deliberately look at situations from more than one perspective – to bring order out of confusion – and to better imagine what "could be".*

As a boost to this capacity, it is recommended that all practitioners should also evolve a capability to engage in *re* and *prosponsive* strategic thinking. Similarly, when engaging in the reframing of strategic thought, the arrival of entrepreneurial serendipity is also always welcome. This is often difficult to evoke, however, especially when the formality, enormity and bureaucratic nature of a corporation inadvertently imposes limitations and constraints on free and open thinking – and imagination. Culture, tradition, situations, industry forces, personalities and complexity are just a few things that impede and adversely (or otherwise) influence the demand for dynamic strategic thinking – and a capacity to reframe. Our conclusion, however, is that sometimes

> *we just need to put the everyday to one side and look at the world, and the things in it from a different perspective.*

An example of reframing at NASA

The US-based National Aeronautics and Space Administration (NASA) – an extreme, low-risk bureaucracy – is now recognised for its ability to do just that. Their experience is discussed in Case example 1.3.

Case example 1.3: Reframing methods of organisational change at the NASA 'Pirate Paradigm'

Even though a capability for reframing evolved from an informal, opportune program, it proved to be highly successful. Referred to as a 'Pirate Paradigm', the approach developed by NASA employees is now an approved, formal way of doing things when employees engage in organisational change projects. The Pirate Paradigm was adopted as a formal system because of its success in the breaking down of the previously 'blocking nature' of its culture. It had as its doctrine a list of 'can do' principles according to Heracleous et al. (2019). Some of the more antagonistic ones are as follows:

- Challenge everything; prepare for the inevitable cynicism, opposition, rumours, false reporting, innuendos, slander.
- Take risks as a rule, not as the exception.
- Eliminate unnecessary timelines, schedules, processes, reviews and bureaucracy.

As illustrated by NASA, an approach to the conduct of Third Wave Strategy, should be supportive of the philosophy of the Pirate Paradigm and its application to future-focused/strategic thinking widely encouraged. Ideally, it should become an ingrained component of an organisation's culture, demeanour and method of learning. It should also be embedded within its ongoing management and control mechanisms, contextualised through its conceptualisation within the construct of the Third Wave Strategy framework. In particular, it should embrace the need for close and open communication with all stakeholders.

Stakeholder Engagement: communicating, motivating and organising for high performance

As the third component of Third Wave Strategy (Figure 1.2), it should be understood that Stakeholder Engagement (Figure 1.6) is important to the success of

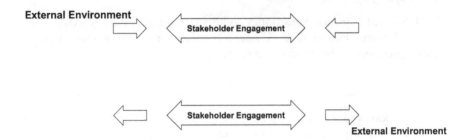

Figure 1.6 Stakeholder Engagement

any change management program, be it reframing, restructuring or, simply, strategising. The term 'Stakeholder Engagement' is used here to describe the way in which the inclusion of all employees, managers, leaders, customers suppliers and others are involved in the strategising process. This includes the activities and interactive events that are undertaken to ensure that the cooperation of all relevant stakeholders occurs up, down and across the organisation. In particular, it is expected that open strategy is a viable method of enabling Stakeholder Engagement within the management and doing of Third Wave Strategy practice.

Formal strategy practice: open strategy practice at the level of a profession

In addressing this concluding component of Third Wave Strategy depicted in Figure 1.2, it should be noted that, increasingly, strategy practitioners will benefit from a formal elevation in the standard of practice to the level of a profession. In promoting such an advance, Whittington et al. (2011) observed that although the idea has merit, it is by nature a "precarious profession". In this sense, the writers observe, it is conducted within a context of open strategy, which makes it, therefore, very much a social enterprise. At the same time, Whittington et al. (2011) observed it is a role that is likely to be highly transient.

The ultimate position of the strategy professional is encapsulated in the role of CSO. This position, however, is often seen as a stepping stone to something else. In many CSOs' minds, no doubt, that something else is the position of CEO. As Whittington et al. suggested, "Strategy is a profession to the extent that it deals with characteristic problems of uncertainty, has common procedures and shares particular bodies of knowledge".

In helping us to develop an understanding of the role of the CSO, Powell and Angwin (2012) identified four 'archetypes' of a (corporate head office level) CSO:

- **Internal consultant:** CSO who adopts a rational approach to strategy formulation

- **Specialist:** CSO chosen for specialised skills not previously held by the organisation
- **Coach:** A facilitator who focuses on strategy formulation with the business units
- **Change agent:** Those who liaise with business units to ensure strategy is formulated with integrity

While their contribution does produce an understanding of the strategy practitioner's role, take note that it is primarily at a head office, corporate level and potentially less representative of the strategy practitioner at a business unit level.

2 Articulating Long Term Strategy

Chapter overview

Everybody can conceptualise the difference between Long and Short Term Strategy. It is surprising, therefore, that a clear articulation of its structure and content is rarely articulated or understood. An explanation of the importance and value of doing so and what it is forms the key message delivered in this chapter.

As the first element in the Third Wave Strategy framework, the notion of Long Term Strategy is explored here from three perspectives. First is an overview of the notional, qualitative statements of intent that explain Purpose, Mission, Vision. Second is its construct, presented in the form of a Strategic Architecture as a representation of the forces of a resource-based Inside Out focus or alternatively that of a market-based Outside In focus. Third is a demonstration of the value of this understanding and how it can be applied in a commercial sense to obtain a competitive advantage, either as 1) an industry follower, or 2) as an industry leader considering the possibility of evolving a combination of each in the form of an Integrated Value System. In its application to SPPD, we demonstrate the makeup of a Strategic Architecture and the way in which Long Term Strategy defines a firm's strategic posturing and options for actions that could follow.

Learning insights

It's impossible to define a meaningful Short Term Strategy (strategic plan) if you don't know what the Long Term Strategy is. To make this task easier, we explore further in this chapter the structure of a Strategic Architecture, what it is, why it is useful and how it works.

In its application to SPPD, a demonstration of the way in which the Strategic Architecture enriches the ambitions of the leadership team is demonstrated and thereby, its contribution to the effectiveness of implementation as they strive to realise their organisational Purpose, Mission, Vision. Specifically, an understanding of the relevance of Long Term Strategy is explored as a potential enabler of Deliberate Disruption and as an essential component of a key element of competitive advantage – that of renewal (transformation) and differentiation.

Accordingly, a demonstration of how Long Term Strategy works as a microsystem is provided. Also demonstrated is its role as an anchor for Short Term Strategy and as a foundation for more radical strategic thinking in the context of a firm's role of industry leader and or follower. This level of thinking also gives cause to SPPD's leadership team to rethink and reinvent their upcoming journey of transformation through a newfound appreciation of the concept of an ambidextrous organisation. In expanding the dimensions of scenario analysis, further insight is also provided into the different pathways that an ambidextrous organisation can follow as it embarks on the journey of transformation and organisational restructuring along the way.

Work plan phase 2: establish details of Long Term Strategy

We proceed in this chapter with a review of content depicted in the second phase of the project work plan presented in Table 2.1. Addressing the concept of Long Term Strategy, the primary elements of the framework that are reviewed here include the collective of Purpose, Mission, Vision and the Strategic Architecture.

Introduction: fundamentals of Long Term Strategy

Such is the derision for expressions of Purpose, Mission, Vision that little attention is given to them in conventional strategy practice. This is surprising given the credence given to these tools awarded by de Vaal (2010), an authority on the conduct of HPOs. If a review of statements of Purpose, Mission, Vision posted on most company's websites is any guide, it can be readily concluded that in reality, few contribute much value to the management of the business. Most are vague and irrelevant to the day-to-day running of the business. It is our observation also that

> *when deployed as formal instruments of importance to stakeholders, statements of Purpose, Mission, Vision are more likely to be filed and forgotten rather than posted on notice boards and the front pages of the intranet, reminding stakeholders of their existence daily.*

Table 2.1 Steps/dates: development and delivery of a strategy and leadership development program at the client organisation: Phase 2

Phase 2: establish details of the Long Term Strategy

1 **Develop, articulate and confirm:** Purpose, Mission, Vision/Long-Term Strategy
2 **Establish Strategic Imperatives**
3 **Build preliminary Strategic Architecture**
4 **Review and revise:** Long Term Strategy, confirm next steps
5 **Rework, frame and reframe:** Strategic Architecture
6 **Evolve strategy development plan**

Prepared mostly at a corporate level, it is reasonable to expect that mission and vision statements at least will be broad-based and generic. At a business unit level, however, practitioners should expect far greater conciseness and clarity while also appreciating their presence as a demonstration of a strength of leadership.

Statements of intent at the business unit level are best deployed for the purposes of leading and managing, engaging and communicating. Ultimately, the content and the way these statements are used will be at the discretion of the organisational leadership and the nature of the culture that those leaders wish to establish or cultivate. One thing that the practitioner can be sure of is that no statement of the future on its own will make any difference to firm performance unless it is followed by good strategy, a strength of leadership, a complementary organisation structure, a sense of ownership and excellence in implementation. So, the message?

> *Long Term Strategy must be guided, informed and aligned with a strong sense of Purpose, Mission, Vision in much the same way that strategy formulation must be aligned with implementation.*

Long Term Strategy: environment and construct of a Strategic Architecture

Statements of Purpose, Mission, Vision provide the foundation for Long Term Strategy. It is likely, however, that the meaning of each will change very little over time. More recent disruption arising from the technology associated with the 4IR and changes in social and political arenas has placed considerable pressure on leaders to ensure that the relevance of each is both sustainable and suitable.

Inventing opportunity as a disrupter: defining points of differentiation

In our introduction to the concept of prosponsive disruption, it must be acknowledged that adaptation is a constant and highly appropriate action to take when the unexpected suddenly happens and the expected finally happens. As observed in our discussion about sponsive strategic change in Chapter 1, however, the threat of ending up in a state of inertia as a result of a submission to adaptation and followership is all too real. This is the case especially in a world of rapid change where there is an increasing risk of being left behind. Sure, there is merit in letting the pioneers lead the way into new markets. Are you sure though that there isn't a bigger risk that a 'wait and see' strategy will be swamped by the whirlwind of a 'winner takes all, big bet move'? In a world where university degrees can be obtained without ever entering a university campus and retailers own no or few physical stores (Amazon, eBay, Alibaba),

> *it is encouraging that ambitious high performance leaders are breaking down preconceived, but often non-existent constraints and industry barriers and accordingly, creating the opportunity for creativity and invention to flourish.*

That is where a reframing of strategy – in the context of Third Wave Strategy practice comes into its own. The question that must now be asked is, "Where to the strategy practitioner facing the assumption that commodity-based firms or plain mature and potentially stale firms such as those operating in chemical, steel and glass industries can develop an opportunity to differentiate their value proposition from competitors?". In other words, "do the choices they make enable them to compete more effectively?" If so, "does the competitive advantage exist in the same way that many other non-commodity businesses or less mature, but agile, dynamic businesses are seemingly able to do?"

In the future, practitioners can expect that new businesses will emerge and they will be agile and dynamic, as they are based on systems-focused service solutions rather than end-to-end processes. Let's explore how the potential for the system solution will impact a commodity classic – a tinned baked beans manufacturer. In the future, it can be speculated that the baked beans manufacturer's conventional basis for transformational growth could be significantly more substantial than cost reduction, product expansion, bolt-on acquisition or packaging variation, as has been a more common practice in the past. As demonstrated in Case example 2.1, it can be speculated that this manufacturer could evolve, either as an independent operator or in partnership with other organisations. This is one that changes in focus and emphasis in order to provide a real opportunity to develop a value-added, systems-based service solution.

Case example 2.1: Leveraging a baked beans cannery's cash flow to establish a super healthy dietary management service offering

Currently, the manufacture and sale of a tin of baked beans can be easily pictured as commencing with the order and receipt of raw materials (tomato sauce, sugar, flavouring and raw haricot [navy] beans) and the processing and packaging of those beans in tin cans and their sale to supermarkets, hotels and cafes. Although prevailing in a state of inertia, they are likely to be an attractive acquisition for one or a few forms of health food or health service providers. Operating at a profit – or close – they would provide a sustainable source of cash flow upon which a transformation could be evolved.

Here's why: Although a simple tinned food product, baked beans represent a fat-free, low-cholesterol protein that are high in nutrition and fibre, low in cost and extremely versatile in application. In this capacity, they could become the core ingredient in the delivery of a broad-based, comprehensive and significantly larger market that operates as a dynamic, customer-focused, health-specific service provider. Inherent competences in the management and processing of the core bean would also be invaluable. The emergent system would operate as a value-added health capability in the form of a new look, integrated health management system. The announcement of the emergence of this new health service could read as follows:

> Following the introduction of online food purchasing and rapid, personalised delivery, we are delighted to introduce a new service, one that provides you with a pre-ordered, diet-specific, pre-prepared meal delivered direct to the location of your choice in a format of your choice. Our range of tasty, bean-based health food options will continue to be available through your nearest supermarket or grocery store. These will include healthy additives, such as avocado, chili and carrot savoury products. Sweet offerings will include pineapple, peach and apple flavouring. As a sustainable production system, our service includes recycling options for our packaging. As a health-specific provider, we offer an individualised dietary regime delivered in various formats that include hot English breakfasts, bean salads and soups and bean-based health bars.
>
> Subscribers to our health management plan will be provided with regular imaginative recipes, as well as recipes for special events, such as Thanksgiving and Christmas. Newsletters will be issued, advising special health tips, along with personalised health reports. The health reports are prepared from information garnered from the combination of our record of our subscribers' food consumption and data generated by their exercise machines and wearable health monitoring equipment. Naturally, we partner with other specialists in the health field, they include other food producers, medical centres, health centres, health insurance agencies, fitness centres and health app developers, as well as holders of medical records (reliant on their permission to do so). Examples of capabilities of the latter sources of data include sleep disorder monitoring equipment, smart hairbrushes that read data from hair samples and smart toilets that monitor the health of your gut.

Think this story is a little farfetched? Let's look next at what Fortune 500 lister Sysco is doing (Case example 2.2).

Case example 2.2: Sysco Corporation: a story of continual organisational transformation

Sysco described itself on its website (Sysco, 2019) as "the global leader in foodservice distribution". Based in Houston, Texas, Sysco "serves more than 650,000 customers our of more than 320 distribution facilities located in 90 different countries". According to the company history on its website, Sysco's line of products includes "fresh and frozen meats, seafood, poultry, fully prepared entrees, produce, canned and dry foods, desserts, imported specialties, paper and disposable items, china and silverware, restaurant and kitchen equipment and supplies, and cleaning supplies". In 2019, Sysco's sales exceeded $60 billion for the first time. In their annual report (Sysco, 2019), Sysco shares their four strategic priorities, which they describe as being their multi-year transformational initiatives, which continue to serve as the road map to the future. They are as follows:

1 **Enriching the customer experience** – Creating the right solutions and services to help our customers be successful and drive additional customer loyalty
2 **Delivering operational excellence** – Leveraging our size and scale to increase levels of productivity across the enterprise
3 **Optimising the business** – Structuring our work to bring incremental value to our customers with a different way of thinking
4 **Activating the power of our people** – Improving upon our strong performance culture to enable our 69,000 associates who help us win in the marketplace each and every day

Today, Sysco encompasses four business groups: Broadline, Specialty Companies, International and Sygma. Each are described as follows:

Broadline: Supplies a full line of food products and a wide variety of non-food products to both independent and chain restaurant customers and other 'away-from-home' locations, such as healthcare and educational facilities.

Specialty Companies: As One Sysco, we ensure every customer everywhere has constant access to our vast selection of specialty foods and supplies. We meet the needs of customers looking for specialised and differentiated products through groups of specialty companies that can be identified under three different categories:

Specialty Produce: Provision of specialty, high-quality and exclusive food products in the areas of meat, seafood and specialist European food imports.

Guest Supply: Supply of specialist hospitality services including bath and bed linens, personal care amenities, guest room accessories, housekeeping supplies, small appliances, furniture, fixtures and other equipment.

Supplies on the Fly: Provide 170,000 foodservice products, including heavy equipment, kitchen supplies, specialty food and pantry staples.

International: The Sysco International Food Group (IFG) is the export specialty division of Sysco. It operates over 30 U.S.-based restaurant chains in over 90 countries. IFG also exports Sysco-branded products to numerous distributors around the world.

Sygma: Made up of 16 operating companies, Sygma distributes a full line of food products and a wide variety of non-food products to chain restaurant customer locations.

In addition to its services, Sysco offers a range of home brand products; these include food, cleaning and related products, four of which exceed $4 billion in sales. It also offers a suite of service solutions that includes technological support to its customers – an example of which is a specialist restaurant-specific technology platform. It also provides a specialty advisory service that is designed to help its customers differentiate and grow their businesses. Referred to as Cutting Edge Solutions, Sysco applies its core competence in research and industry knowledge to "create distinctive and relevant concepts to consumers" (Sysco, 2019).

In the Sysco 2019 annual report, chairman, president and CEO Tom Bené indicated that he was thinking a lot more deeply about strategy than the high-level content presented earlier would suggest. Demonstrating an orientation towards Third Wave Strategy practice, he advised,

> "In fiscal 2019, we gathered leaders from around the company with the goal of building clarity around the new realities of our operating environment, and the need to have an agile culture where we can elevate our company to even higher levels of customer focus and performance. As we look to the future, we have plans in place beginning in fiscal 2020 to help us broaden this mindset and deliver the transformational change required to grow and deliver strong results." (Sysco Annual Report, 2019)

When Sysco was formed, its fact sheet suggested, 77% of its business was associated with frozen foods distribution. Dry and canned items amounted to only 17% of total sales, with disposable and other non-food products contributing 6%. Its primary method of growth has been through continual acquisition. Today, it boasts that it is a "global leader in selling, marketing and distributing food and non-food products to restaurants, healthcare and educational facilities, lodging establishments and other customers around the world".

It is reasonable to suggest, therefore, that there is some merit to the baked beans promise of transformation and that even a quasi-integrated systems perspective such as that demonstrated by Sysco (Case example 2.2) can pay big dividends. As an outcome of that massive acquisition drive, Sysco is today an HPO. It should be noted however, that not all transformation journeys will commence from the worst case scenario of a state of inertia. As discussed in Case example 2.3, Orica Mining Services is an example of a commodity-based producer that wasn't in a state of inertia before commencing a journey of transformation. Orica was first listed on the Australian stock exchange following the international break up of ICI Plc. in 2008. ICI was previously known as Imperial Chemical Industries. Today, Orica operates in a state of Agile Adaptation; it is still keen to transform apparently, in the short term at least, to a level of Dynamic Adaptation, purely through the introduction of digital technology.

Case example 2.3: Orica Mining Services: a hyper – high performance Integrated Value System

The Australian company Orica Mining Services' core business is the provision of blast services to mining companies throughout the world. Orica doesn't just deliver sticks of dynamite in big boxes to mine sites. Its service offering includes the transportation of raw material ingredients to the mine in one purpose-built vehicle that carries enough chemicals to ignite a number of explosions at the mine site. The chemical mixture that creates the blast is prepared on site and then installed into prepared holes at predesignated points around the mine. The driver of the vehicle then orchestrates, manages and initiates the deposit of explosives and ignition of the blast.

Orica's service enhances the value of the product offering that would otherwise be a range of commodity chemicals to mining companies. Even with a bundled service offering, it was still difficult for Orica to differentiate itself from its competitors. That was until May 2015, when Orica announced the appointment of Alberto Calderon as managing director. Although Calderon faced numerus challenges, he also had access to a suite of untapped digital technology initiatives that had been identified by his predecessor, Ian Smith.

Smith had spent some time establishing a strategy that would see an upgrade to Orica's SAP Enterprise Resource Planning (ERP) system. It would deliver efficiencies through its expansion all the way across the company's global network. Rather than a broad-based, global roll-out of an ERP system alone, however, Calderon saw the opportunity to rationalise the 15 programs that Smith had initiated. In rationalising the investment in the technology roll-out, Calderon sought to capitalise on the opportunity to deploy advanced digital technology that would deliver a game-changing capability in three key areas: wireless blasting, digital technologies that collect and analyse data from drilling and explosions and the vehicles that deliver the newly invented innovations.

Essentially, Calderon boasted, this new technology could "collect and analyse in real time, data from drilling and explosions, and the (previously mentioned) innovative vehicles that deliver that game-changing service" (Stevens, 2018). As a business that was otherwise condemned to follow the usual bulk commodity path that sees firms compete solely on price, Calderon's objective was to not only introduce measures of efficiency and effectiveness but also "offer (Orica) the opportunity of long- term trans- formation" (Stevens, 2019) to that of a supplier of 'smart mine blasting'.

In just two years, the results were in. Stevens (2019) was delighted to report, "Orica has secured increased market share in its biggest and most mature markets through its patented suite of intelligent drilling equipment and first-generation wireless blasting technology, as well as its live data processing and digital geotechnical monitoring capacities". Ultimately, Stevens noted, Orica has succeeded in a transformation from a basic blasting-based mining services company to that of one of the mining world's most informative and complex mining service providers.

Overall, Orica has demonstrated how well-informed, less constrained indus- try participants are free to decide their own future within or beyond prevailing industry rules. Any ambitions beyond the status quo for commodity-based busi- nesses will always be threatened by a fear of constraint from an abundance of external market, industry and environmental forces. Such forces will inevitably impose favourable and/or unfavourable influences on firm performance at any time. It is our view that just as new technology arrives in open markets – and as cognitive awareness of actions taken by incumbent strategy practitioners to define new boundaries also occurs – so too will new business opportunities emerge.

Ultimately, strategy practitioners can expect to see the rationalisation of entire industries initiated through the conduct of Green Shoot, accelerated Deliberate Disruption. The notion of Green Shoot Strategy and its application to practice is discussed further in Chapter 6 of this book.

Construct of Long Term Strategy: establishing a Strategic Architecture

As an illustration of the construct of a Strategic Architecture and an approach to its construction, you are invited to imagine yourself as John Jenkins, a recent graduate from cabinet-making school who is planning to start a furniture man- ufacturing business. Your journey is described as follows and is based on the Strategic Architecture presented in Figure 2.1.

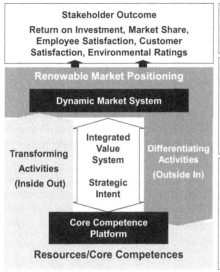

The diagram on the right contains the following text:

Stakeholder Outcomes: Articulation of vision, mission and desired financial, social and ecological outcomes from the business and key purpose in setting a strategy.

Outside In

Renewable Market Position: Bespoke, branded and high-spec furniture; subsequent enhancement can lead to development of a Dynamic Market System

Differentiating Activities: Local timber, handmade to unique design

Inside out

Resources/Core Competences: Premises, trained staff, plant and equipment, administrative and operating systems. When combined it is possible to establish a Core Competence Platform

Transforming Activities: Develops strategy, secures premises, acquires tools and equipment and other resources

The left diagram contains: Stakeholder Outcome — Return on Investment, Market Share, Employee Satisfaction, Customer Satisfaction, Environmental Ratings; Renewable Market Positioning; Dynamic Market System; Transforming Activities (Inside Out); Integrated Value System; Differentiating Activities (Outside In); Strategic Intent; Core Competence Platform; Resources/Core Competences

Figure 2.1 An example of a Strategic Architecture of relevance to an entrepreneur starting a furniture manufacturing business

Constructing a Strategic Architecture: John Jenkins Furniture

Before any form of strategy or planning can take place, it is essential for you, the entrepreneur, to understand the fundamentals at least of Purpose, Mission, Vision. Details required should include an articulation of company policy, operational infrastructure and desired financial, social and ecological boundaries you will need to define once it is up and running. An understanding and articulation of the financial and nonfinancial goals and objectives should also be established.

Strategy is the one thing that will remain prominent and future focused for the life of the business. It is useful, therefore, to understand and communicate why it is needed and how it will help other stakeholders. Depending on the expected complexity and extent of ambition set for your business, it will also be useful to understand how you will approach the market. It could be as a marketing-oriented (Outside In) business or a resource-focused (Inside Out) business or both. No doubt the targets you set will, in terms of financial, ecological and social orientations, have a strong influence on your decision.

In adding an extra dimension to your thinking, you will have observed that in the image of the Strategic Architecture presented in Figure 2.1, two new dimensions are added which combine to form an Integrated Value System. This system is in turn made up of a Dynamic Market System and a Core Competence Platform. Each of these are described as follows.

Integrated Value System

Such a system can be can be readily identified in the Orica (Case example 2.3) and Sysco (Case example 2.2) case studies. This is a system that is evolved from the physical alignment of an Outside In, customer-focused Dynamic Market System and an Inside Out, resource-focused Core Competence Platform. A Utopian version of such a value system is described as follows:

> *An Integrated Value System has the capacity to support both an inimitable resource base and a compelling renewable and impregnable market system upon which an organisation can establish an unassailable point of differentiation.*

Our definition of value in this context refers to the optimisation of efficiency and effectiveness in the resource base in a form and format consistent with measures of best possible price and quality in the market, assessed through the eyes of the customer. In our development of this system, each element is defined as follows:

Dynamic Market System

This is a network of related service offerings centred around the mainstay market position. The market presence that Sysco (Case example 2.2) established is an example of such a system. According to Encyclopaedia of American Industries Reference for Business, Sysco provides a range of related items that include "food and related products and services to approximately 390,000 restaurants, schools, hospitals, nursing homes, hotels, businesses, and other foodservice customers. Restaurant customers account for fully two-thirds of revenues". Although not specifically designed as a market system, the opportunity to do so exists and could deliver significant advantage. Orica also demonstrate such a system through its combination of services to mining companies. Their service definition started with a full service mine blasting operation supported with professional advice about that process. Following their investment in digital technology, however, the Dynamic Market System was boosted by the addition of comprehensive and detailed operating data. That information provided the means for its customers to significantly improve their efficiency and effectiveness in the operation of their mines and the way they deploy Orica's operations at the same time.

Core Competence Platform

This is a mechanism that combines tangible and intangible resources (and core competences) into a single platform. As witnessed in the Sysco case study, a Core Competence Platform of value to the restaurant industry especially can be identified in its physical supply chain infrastructure, its associated supporting technology and its management- and industry-specific know-how.

A similar platform can be identified in the Orica case study (Case example 2.3), now enhanced by the newly established digital technology platform. By adding wireless blasting and data analytics to its already integrated blast services and advice, Orica has effectively built a Core Competence Platform that enabled it to steal a significant and sustainable competitive advantage in its marketplace.

Both Sysco and Orica exhibit features of an Integrated Value System through their combination of a Dynamic Market System and Core Competence Platform. An illustrative Strategic Architecture incorporating an Integrated Value System for Sysco appears as Figure 2.2.

In our review of the John Jenkins Strategic Architecture, our review commences at the top with an analysis of Stakeholder Outcomes.

Stakeholder Outcomes:

Of fundamental concern is an articulation of desired outcomes from the business; it is an issue of relevance to all stakeholders.

> ***Stakeholder Outcomes are the desired objectives set for the business that will satisfy the expectations of all stakeholders, such as owners, other shareholders, employees, suppliers and customers.***

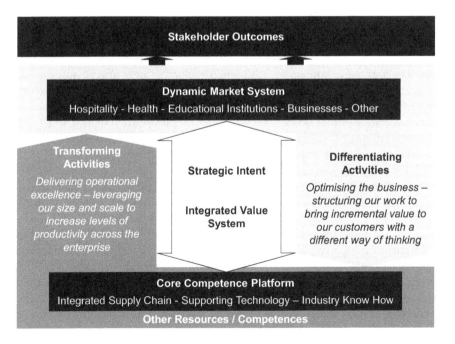

Figure 2.2 An illustrative Strategic Architecture incorporating an Integrated Value System at Sysco

In that articulation it is expected that you include the financial and nonfinancial goals and objectives that you will wish to obtain for your business. Examples of Stakeholder Outcomes are rates of return (on assets, sales), market share, employee satisfaction, customer satisfaction and environmental ratings. When setting targets for such outcomes, it is advisable to be aware that the goals, objectives and targets that are set in the short term may not be the same as those desired in the long term. In the setting of Long Term Strategy, therefore, targets could be much higher (or lower) than the level of those established in the short term Strategy Narrative. Return on sales, for example, may be 5% for the first year, 15% in the second and from there on the amount included in the Strategic Architecture, say, 20%.

Having rigorously reviewed strategic alternatives with high-level Stakeholder Outcomes in mind, you must now decide whether to proceed with the establishment of your business, or get a job!

Core elements of the Strategic Architecture

For most start-ups and entrepreneurs, as well as in corporations, new CEOs commence their envisioning of Long Term Strategy with an understanding and articulation of their proposed transforming activities. In reality, however, all elements of the Strategic Architecture come in to play in this analysis as ideas about differentiation, resource sets and market opportunities flash backwards and forwards in the entrepreneur's and/or corporate CEO's mind.

In the case of a corporation, the notion of transformation is all too often focused on a short term review of the cost structure and the pursuit of a natural inclination to reduce it. As you will have observed this was originally the case with Jenny Wong at T-wI, SPPD. This focus, though, is not always the best place to start. As as you appreciated when evaluating new insight into the use of scenario analysis, the immediacy of cost reduction offers short term results but not necessarily long term survival – or thrival. Nonetheless, cost-reduction initiatives are deemed popular by new CEOs because they represent a sharp demonstration of their strength of leadership; they are readily measurable and deliver an immediate impact on bottom-line (profit) performance.

When launching on a transformation journey, for better or for worse, it is often the case that cost and resource rationalisation are the key objectives. Such actions provide a useful means to finance the transformation journey as well. An example is Ford Motor Company, where newly appointed CEO Jim Hackett maintained a view of cost management that is more in the context of resource redeployment and asset utilisation, especially as a means to reduce working capital, than cost reduction alone. Having launched a massive organisational transformation program in 2018 (Ford, 2018), Hackett is expected to build an advanced technology-focused Core Competence Platform, similar in concept to the integrated technology-based supply chain operated at Amazon. As we saw in our discussion about Ford in our first volume of Corporate Strategy (Remastered) I, Hackett is endeavoring to establish a Core Competence Platform as part of a journey of transformation. He refers to Fords version of such a construct as a 'mobility platform'. His vision: "design smart vehicles for a smart world" (Ford, 2018).

These observations are of relevance to your analysis of the Strategic Architecture in your role as the founder of John Jenkins Furniture. A good place to start is with the position identified as an Inside Out orientation made up of transforming activities and a resource base.

Transforming activities (improving resources)

In our use of the term 'transforming activities', we adapt the definition of 'Dynamic Capabilities', described by Ambrosini and Bowman (2009) as being those activities that "alter the resource base". In their paper, the authors identified three levels of transforming activities that relate to managers' perceptions of relevance to our discussion. They are:

1   **Incremental transforming activities:** Those activities concerned with the continuous improvement of the firm's resource base
2   **Renewing transforming activities:** Those activities that refresh, adapt and augment the resource base
3   **Regenerative transforming activities:** Those activities which impact, not only the firm's resource base but also its current set of transforming activities – that is, the activities that change the way the firm changes its resource base

Each of these formal dimensions carry clear notions of continual learning and continual performance improvement. Uncoincidentally, both are also key components of Hyper – HPOs and, importantly, practitioners of a Third Wave Strategy philosophy. Beyond setting your strategy and business plan, and the emphasis contained therein, long term transforming activities that you choose to include in the Strategic Architecture will no doubt be related in some way to the activities of organisational learning and continual performance improvement.

To describe the concept of transforming activities in your role as a furniture-making entrepreneur, you can be congratulated for completing your first transforming activity – that is, the acquisition of your primary resource: a professional level of skill in furniture making. As the first step in the foundation of your business's resource base, the next question you will be required to address is, "What do I need to add to my resource base to effectively differentiate my business in order to compete in my chosen industry/market?"

The answer lies in part in your choice of transforming activities. It is unhelpful to select a resource base that you can maintain, improve or leverage for future gain, for example, without the presence of a suite of transforming activities that are in your power to control. In this context, you will agree that transforming activities will become an entrenched component of Long Term Strategy. To decide what they ultimately should be, you will need to understand the setting of both your Long Term and Short Term Strategy content. In the short term, objectives will likely involve the design and location of premises, the way you will maintain and renew your premises, tools and equipment and the identification and acquisition of any other strategic assets (Amit and Schoemaker, 1993) that may provide a point of uniqueness and the foundation of a sustainable competitive advantage.

Similar to furniture manufactures are consumer goods manufacturers. An example is Lego, a specialist in the design and manufacture of plastic toy bricks and themed designed kits. Lego's survival relies on skills in design and precision engineering; its thrival relies on it being in a position to improve those skills constantly. A fundamental component of its strategy, therefore, is its education, nurturing and encouragement of specialist production designers upon whom the mass production and, thereby, the success of Lego's entire range is dependent. Add to this the capacity to operate a precision manufacturing capability – a difficult task when production capability demands a competence in the management of a material (plastic) that is malleable and difficult to handle. Include also, rather surprisingly, a capacity to churn out prepared meals – a side addition to IKEA's business, which has grown beyond all preconceived expectations.

Organisational resources (strategic assets)

For a number of years now, the focus for strategy has been placed primarily on the firm's resource base. As suggested previously, this has been realised through a relentless pursuit of cost reduction and associated improvements in efficiency and effectiveness. As the proprietor of John Jenkins Furniture, it is recommended you apply a more strategic approach to your resource management than that. Not forgetting of course that cost management is always important, as is the maintenance and management of the entire resource base. In making your decision, you must decide what your primary source of competitive advantage and primary source of growth will be.

The resources you choose could include tangible assets, such as specialist skills and qualifications of staff, use of advanced technology in manufacturing and the nature of the administrative operating systems you deploy. It could also include any number of intangible assets, such as brand, reputation and knowledge (in the form of design skills or timber processing and management). Amongst these options, any insights into the nature of the core competences you wish to evolve will be useful, as would the construct of a Core Competence Platform. The term "core competence" describes attributes that are "difficult and (ideally) impossible to copy" (Prahalad and Hamel, 1990). Examples of core competences applicable to a furniture manufacturer could include a uniqueness in furniture design, knowledge of timber treatments, processing of timber or steel or the design of fabrics used to cover the timber or steel skeleton.

A Core Competence Platform can rapidly become an integral component of a furniture-making business. Such a platform would include a variety of options that could include the uniqueness of product manufacture and design, a tailored inventory management, tracking and invoicing system, as well as some form of customer relationship management system. To be classified as a Core Competence Platform, it will need to combine two or three core competences to provide a foundation from which further development and growth

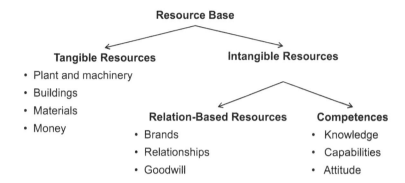

Figure 2.3 Illustrative content of typical resource base (strategic assets)

can evolve. Ikea found such a platform when an employee apparently sawed a leg off a table when their customer couldn't fit it into their car. From there, IKEA evolved a Core Competence Platform of modular design, flat pack construction offering easy transportation, and unique product designs. A summary of strategically oriented descriptions of firm resources that will contribute to a business's capacity to survive and thrive is illustrated in Figure 2.3.

Our journey around the Strategic Architecture continues, this time from an Outside In orientation made up of renewable market positioning and differentiating activities.

Renewable market positioning

In broad terms, market positioning is all about identifying and benefiting from a unique market position. Energy drink manufacturer Red Bull is a widely recognised brand, as is the sportswear manufacturer Nike. Both of these organisation's strategies are focused entirely on the market positioning component of an Outside In strategy. Both exhibit product profiles that are essentially representative of a commodity. In order to maintain their appeal, Red Bull and Nike associate their brand with an evolving (and revolving) suite of sports people and teams. Red Bull favours high-risk, spectacular sporting codes, such as car and aeroplane racing, to attract attention in its pursuit of market share. Nike favours high-performance athletes in field and track, swimming and similar individual sporting activities.

In the second wave strategy era and beyond, strategy theory was focused very much on markets and market share as the key driver of a sustainable competitive advantage. The essence of this focus was an assessment of the attractiveness of industries and markets that the firm could explore and exploit in order to excel. It has been an expectation for some time that industry characteristics hold a strong influence over firm-specific strategy. For now, it is sufficient to understand that a market orientation is focused on things we *have*. Examples are market share, market position and customer segments. From the mid-1960s and well into the mid-1980s, market share and market positioning were *the* primary focus for strategy theory. An illustration of Porter's (1980) basis for determining a competitive advantage in markets, for example, appears in Figure 2.4.

We refer to the term 'renewable market position' in recognition of the fact that in today's fast-moving and uncertain world it will in all likelihood be appropriate to continually review and renew your positioning and, in fact, every other aspect of strategy on a continual basis. In our most recent deliberations, the concept of a renewable market position is elevated to the next level. As discussed previously, this is the identification of the notion of a Dynamic Market System.

The two market focused organisations we referred to previously, Red Bull and Nike are recognised for their prowess as single product, market focused operators. Red Bull benefits from an apparent health aspect of its drink product and adds to that positivity with an association with high-performance sports. Nike, on the other hand, has only its brand to rely on as most of its product range is readily copied by others. Its approach to association with high achievement in the sports arena still contributes significantly to its brand recognition and, thereby, point of differentiation. Both Red Bull and Nike are so successful in doing what they are doing, that the idea and attraction of a broader based, Dynamic Market System would unlikely be of interest – or would it?

In the case of John Jenkins Furniture, therefore, it is probably more appropriate to establish a competitive market position that will put you in a positive financial position before worrying about the establishment of a Dynamic Market System. Having said that, a knowledge of its existence will inform your

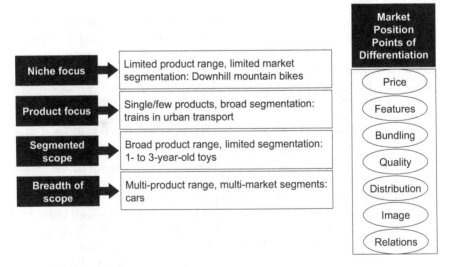

Figure 2.4 Points of differentiation in a market-focused strategy

decision making as the opportunity to establish such a system could emerge quite quickly. This will play out immediately as you make a choice between establishing your own sales showroom and network as an alternative to selling direct existing furniture retailers. With your own showroom, you will have total control but lower opportunity to achieve high volume sales. As a provider to existing retailers, you are putting control of your distribution capabilities in the hands of others. This option, though, is likely to reach higher volume sales than you could reach alone, at least in the short term. Sales would be realised much more quickly but would be realised at much lower margins.

Differentiating activities (differentiation)

The idea of differentiation is to identify those things (activities) that an organisation can '*do*' to differentiate itself from competitors (Porter, 1996). A good example of a firm that competes through differentiating activities is US-based Southwest Airlines. With a focus on friendly service, speed and a flying pattern of point-to-point departures, the authors of *Blue Ocean Strategy*, Kim and Mauborgne (2006), describe Southwest's competitive advantage as being "the speed of a plane at the price of a car, whenever you need it". In essence, Southwest is not much more than a low-cost airline. It does, however, differentiate itself from other airlines that fly hub to hub by running its planes from city to city. It also offers lower prices than mainstream airlines and a superior level of customer service while only providing on-board purchase of meals. It offers no airport lounges and no choice of class other than coach.

In your role as founder of John Jenkins Furniture, it is recommended that your evaluation of an Outside In perspective of strategy should include the identification of clear acts of differentiation. Examples of differentiation in the service you provide could be the supply of locally sourced timber that is handmade to your customers' unique specifications, use of exclusive designs from a highly accomplished designer and a bespoke service.

Articulating Long Term Strategy at T-wI, SPPD

In her new role as SPPD Division Managing Director, Jenny Wong admits that prior to her meeting with her corporate strategy colleague, Alicia Manning, her first reaction was to set immediate strategic objectives that focused on cost-reduction initiatives alone. Under Alicia's direction, the Long Term Strategy that was reflected in a preliminary and illustrative Strategic Architecture designed specifically for SPPD should include a Strategic Intent of *global supremacy in security printing and packaging solutions*. An illustration of the first-pass Strategic Architecture and the Strategic Imperatives that are included in its content appear in Figure 2.5.

Regrettably, when presented in this concise format, it became obvious to Jenny and Alicia that this strategy had proposed nothing more than restricting and entrapping SPPD in a quadrant of Inertia as depicted in the sponse matrix illustrated in Figure 0.2. Similarly, she realised some of the Strategic Imperatives,

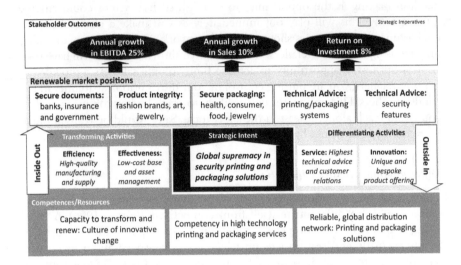

Figure 2.5 A first pass Strategic Architecture of relevance to SPPD

such as "high-quality manufacturing and supply", did not contribute a lot to a philosophy of renewal or even an enhancement to their competitive advantage; in fact, she realised, it hardly meant anything in all reality. Accordingly, further review and discussion with the leadership team was deemed necessary and urgent.

Having considered a range of possible options as a result of those discussions, the decision was made to adopt a more aggressive approach to their plans for transformation. Although the cost focus remained a fundamental requirement, the leadership team now resolved to look at ways to improve the longer-term outlook. These included options leading to better cost management, as well as suggestions for further investment. When seeking to provide as much clarification about their future as possible, the leadership team also resolved to establish statements of Purpose, Mission, Vision. Results of their deliberations are listed as follows:

> **Purpose:** Bring peace of mind to those who entrust us with the security of their high-value goods, chattels, services, documents and artefacts.
>
> **Mission:** Our mission is to provide advanced, high technology and non-discriminatory services to all our customers in a way that represents the veracity of commerce, individual integrity, secure mobility and delivery of support services.
>
> **Intent:** We will act as trusted and discrete professionals in the printing, packaging and delivery of specialty security and advice in the product categories of secure documents, goods and services; the storage and transference of high-value goods; the delivery of protective security services; and the authentication of documents and high-value artefacts.

Values: At a fundamental operating level, T-wI, SPPD will apply the highest standards of moral fortitude, codes of conduct and values to the way in which we interact with all our stakeholders.

Vision: To become the global provider of choice in the delivery of high-security products and services provided to customers of any size, in any location and by any means.

Although needing to lean a little harder on the corporate office for financial funding, the SPPD leadership team opted to engage in options whose primary objective would be to improve the efficiency and effectiveness of core business through higher productivity. This meant that they should

- set cost-reduction targets – and stick to them;
- invest in technology aimed at the introduction of automation and elimination of wasteful resources in manufacturing processes, as well as back-office support;
- satisfy growth requirements through investment in innovative digitalisation and a search for complimentary 'bolt-on' acquisitions designed to grow market share in existing business areas; and
- meet criticism of a lack of concern for the environment by resolving to address and publicise their intent to address this issue as a priority.

Strategic priorities for SPPD

As an outcome from their early discussions, Jenny and Alicia also chose to obtain a greater alignment between its resources and the market positioning aspect of their strategy. Their desire was, in fact, to place a greater focus on customer centricity overall. To do this, they sought to spruce up the Strategic Imperatives identified in this area of the Strategic Architecture. Somewhat shy of entertaining the idea of developing a Dynamic Market System, they resolved to commence a restructuring of the division that would favour the idea of market segmentation at the very least. This would see it split into three different market-focused service definitions: those of packaging, security features and printing.

Next, Alicia sought to reflect the format of its new structure in a revised Strategic Architecture. The result is illustrated in Figure 2.6. To get to this level of detail, the executive team spent some time in workshops that required self-reflection, reviewing of their scenario analysis, discussion and debate. The use of the body of knowledge that was presented from the scenario analysis played a big part in enabling their 'big picture' learning to continue and strategic discussions to progress.

Although a supporter of engagement and openness, Jenny felt it was too early to entertain the idea of formally applying the principles of open strategy practice across the organisation. There was a strong sense of urgency about the determination of this strategy, and she didn't have time for any niceties. The future of the business was on the line.

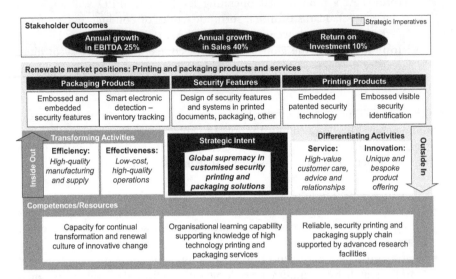

Figure 2.6 Revised Strategic Architecture for SPPD Long Term Strategy

Alicia conducts further research

Although confident of their progress, Alicia was concerned that the overall direction of the Long Term Strategy she had helped Jenny define was still not sufficiently innovative or aggressive. Nor was it, she thought, overly strategic, especially when she considered the kind of technology she was now starting to learn about from her information technology colleagues. It was with great delight that they had alerted her to the promise of digitalisation and the broader aspects that made up the technological phenomenon often referred to as the 4IR. Alicia resolved there and then that she would continue to explore the means to identify a more dynamic and potentially more ambitious multidimensional view of the future. To this end, she was conscious of the need to break down long-held mental models of 'what is' and instead learn to envisage images of what 'could be'. A broader depth of scenario analysis, she hoped, would encourage further dialogue and strengthen the depth of discussion within the SPPD leadership team.

Adding strategic postures to scenario analysis

In her search to identify the means to develop a better perspective of SPPD strategy, Alicia was keen to develop a deep and far-reaching understanding of what was possible. Much more, she thought, could and should be obtained from scenario analysis than a short term response to an obvious need for long term change. In exploring a quest for a meaningful transformation, Alicia introduced results from her own research (Hunter, 2001) to Jenny. She advised her that *those organisations that entered a program of organisational transformation and renewal with a clear understanding of what they wanted to become, were far better positioned and more likely to realise a positive outcome than those that were merely adopting a random cost-reduction program based on a vague hope that no more needed to be done.*

In seeking an added dimension to their scenario analysis, Alicia referred to Courtney, author of *2020 Foresight* (Courtney, 2001). In his book, Courtney illuminates Ansoff's assumption that content deployed in traditional strategic planning paradigms is highly predictable. Through his deliberations, Courtney observed that although the foundations of formal strategic/corporate planning rely on certainty about the future, a true understanding of certainty can only be realised 'by degrees'. To this end, Courtney observed,

If the future is 100% certain, planning is a viable strategy tool. Conversely, if the future is 100% uncertain, preparing a strategic plan is a waste of time.

In reality, the future will never be 100% certain or 100% uncertain. In the middle lies degrees of certainty and uncertainty. His idea, therefore, was to use scenario analysis to provide insight in an environment which as suggested previously is based on possible, but not probable, outcomes. As a rule, the greater the uncertainty, the greater the value practitioners can derive from the 'stories of the future' that emerge from scenario analysis.

Courtney (2001) concluded it appropriate to apply different postures to the representation of strategic change. Postures, he suggests, are "definitions of the Strategic Intent relative to the future of the industry within which the corporation operates". In our interpretation of Courtney's view, we apply our definition of Strategic Intent, which was described previously as "a definition of the fundamental and underlying purpose of Long Term Strategy but not the underlying purpose of the organisation".

Interestingly, Alicia observed that Courtney's notion of strategic postures and associated actions are fully aligned with the characteristics of sponse that were depicted in the sponse matrix illustrated in Figure 0.2. So far, our commentary on sponse has related purely to an assessment of 'what is' – that is, an assessment of the characteristics of a sponse quadrant within which a firm *currently* resides. When creating strategy, however, strategy practitioners are actively concerned with the Strategic Intent or, in other words, the quadrant within which a firm would *choose* to reside. Few businesses, other than those operating in environments of extreme certainty, for example, are likely to aspire to knowingly maintain a presence within a state of inertia – as is the case with SPPD. Even in more advanced states of sponse, as demonstrated by Orica (Case example 2.3), the desire is usually to progress towards a more positive trajectory of high performance than the reverse.

For strategy formulation purposes, therefore, a transformation from one less positive quadrant of the sponse matrix to another is the most likely objective of the strategy practitioner. That is why a strategy that focuses on transformational

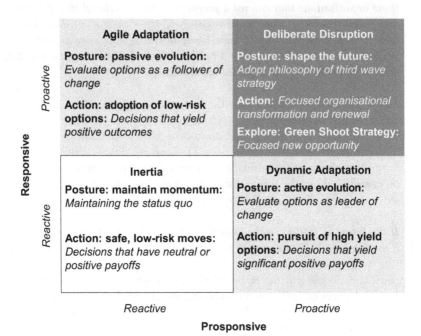

Figure 2.7 Dimension of the sponse matrix reflecting states of sponse and associated actions at SPPD

change is generally the optimal choice. An analysis of strategic change 'postures' that will contribute to our understanding of ways to deliver positive strategic change is illuminated by Courtney (2001). His insight into perspectives of strategic postures and corresponding actions offer a loose but plausible correlation with each quadrant of the sponse matrix demonstrated in Figure 2.7. Each are discussed as follows:

1   Sponse quartile: Inertia

Posture: maintain momentum: In one sense, this position relates to a business that needs no additional momentum and can exist (or not) by maintaining the status quo. Typically, this company will deploy low-impact transformations, such as an intensive focus on costs, skills maintenance and low-level marketing campaigns. An example is an opera or ballet company that survives on brand recognition, a small supply of resources (dancers) and the goodwill of supporters of the arts. In another sense, it is organisations that are similar to SPPD. They simply don't know how to compete or change and are trapped in a state of inertia.

Actions taken: safe, low risk moves: Decisions that have positive or, at worst, neutral pay-offs. They typically will carry low risks but high expectations of positive pay-offs in any scenario.

2   **Sponse quartile: Agile Adaptation**

Posture: passive evolution: A strategy that is representative of an active *follower* of transformation. An example is the entire automotive industry that was forced by a single company, Tesla, to introduce or transform to a new source of energy in their product line-ups: electricity.

Actions taken: adoption of low-risk options: Uptake of decisions that deliver a significant positive pay-off in some outcomes and a (small) negative outcome in others. Results are certain because this company is likely following a transformational path already taken by others.

3   **Sponse quartile: Dynamic Adaptation**

Posture: active evolution: Strategy that is representative of an active *leader* of transformation. An example is again Tesla. It went against the entire automotive industry to develop electricity storage as a source of energy.

Actions taken: pursuit of high yield options: Invention and uptake of opportunities that will yield significant positive outcomes. Participants taking this action should accept that some will inevitably result in (small) negative pay-offs or losses in others. Outcomes are uncertain as Tesla found – having recorded many financial losses (Waters, 2019) because it is a company leading change in ways not yet taken by others.

4   **Sponse quartile: Deliberate Disruption**

Posture: shape the future: Capitalise on serendipitous opportunity to transform and renew existing business, as well as to explore the notion of Green Shoot Strategy (Chapter 6) to evolve new business. Clear examples are Apple, Google and Amazon, who have each designed and invented their own future and new business spin-offs.

Actions taken: Deliberate Disruption: Focused strategies with positive pay-offs in one or more scenarios and acceptance of a negative effect on others. Outcomes can be very uncertain because companies in this quadrant are doing things that are unique. Apple, for example, has recorded huge successes; at the same time, its Newton Message Pad PDA and the first version of Apple Maps in iOS 6 failed miserably.

The linking of methodologies described earlier requires understanding and continued evaluation and reevaluation of outcomes. Should the postures adopted end up conflicting with each other, things will become very interesting. A decision to engage in a Deliberate Disruption by an organisation wallowing in a state of Inertia, for example, will likely be overly ambitious initially. In contrast, an organisation residing in a state of inertia that chooses to simply continue safe, low-risk moves is unlikely to do much more than remain that way indefinitely or simply wither on the vine.

Application of scenario-based strategic postures to SPPD

An application of these matchups was of great interest to Alicia and Jenny. The matrix they subsequently chose to adopt as an outcome from similar analysis conducted at SPPD provided them with a foundation for further review and consideration, as illustrated in Figure 2.7.

A new perspective of strategy and a revised Strategic Architecture for SPPD

Jenny's fear that a focus on cost reduction and random bolt-on acquisitions alone was short-sighted was now confirmed. There was also a risk, she thought, that any incorrect conclusions could seriously impede the introduction of long term ambitions she held for SPPD. Armed with insight from the revised sponse matrix in the context of their scenario analysis, she started to wonder about the value of her intent to improve efficiency and effectiveness alone. This required SPPD to

- invest in technology aimed at developing markets of the future using 'smart' packaging solutions, and
- search for acquisitions designed to grow market share in existing business areas.

As a result of her review and reassessment of her original decision, Jenny now admits she and her team had underestimated the

- capacity of existing technology to effectively deliver improvements in product capability, operating performance and customer service;
- extent of opportunity that could be created through the invention of new products, markets and industries altogether;
- strength of SPPD executive teams' capacity to manage a transformation of the organisation; and
- extent of urgency required in the development of a response to the increasing social pressure to reduce the use of plastics by environmentalists.

By adding components of sponsiveness and dimensions of strategic posturing to the foregoing observations, a new picture of the scenarios depicting the potential for a prosperous, long term future of SPPD emerged. An analysis was completed. The result is illustrated as Figure 2.8.

Jenny explored with Alicia their options to lead T-wI's transformation to a vibrant Hyper – HPO through the conduct of a pilot program at SPPD. Favouring an orientation towards Scenario 3 EcoTech, Jenny and the team soon resolved that they would embrace the idea of investing in technology to improve productivity. Because of its relatively early stage of development, they elected to adopt a cautious approach to its introduction. At the same time, they sought to signal to their customers and the community in general that they were conscious of the need to improve service quality and become more concerned about the environment and societal health in general.

In defining the latest developments in this transformation program, therefore, they resolved that they would evaluate the option of building a Core Competence Platform upon which their newly defined ambitions could be based.

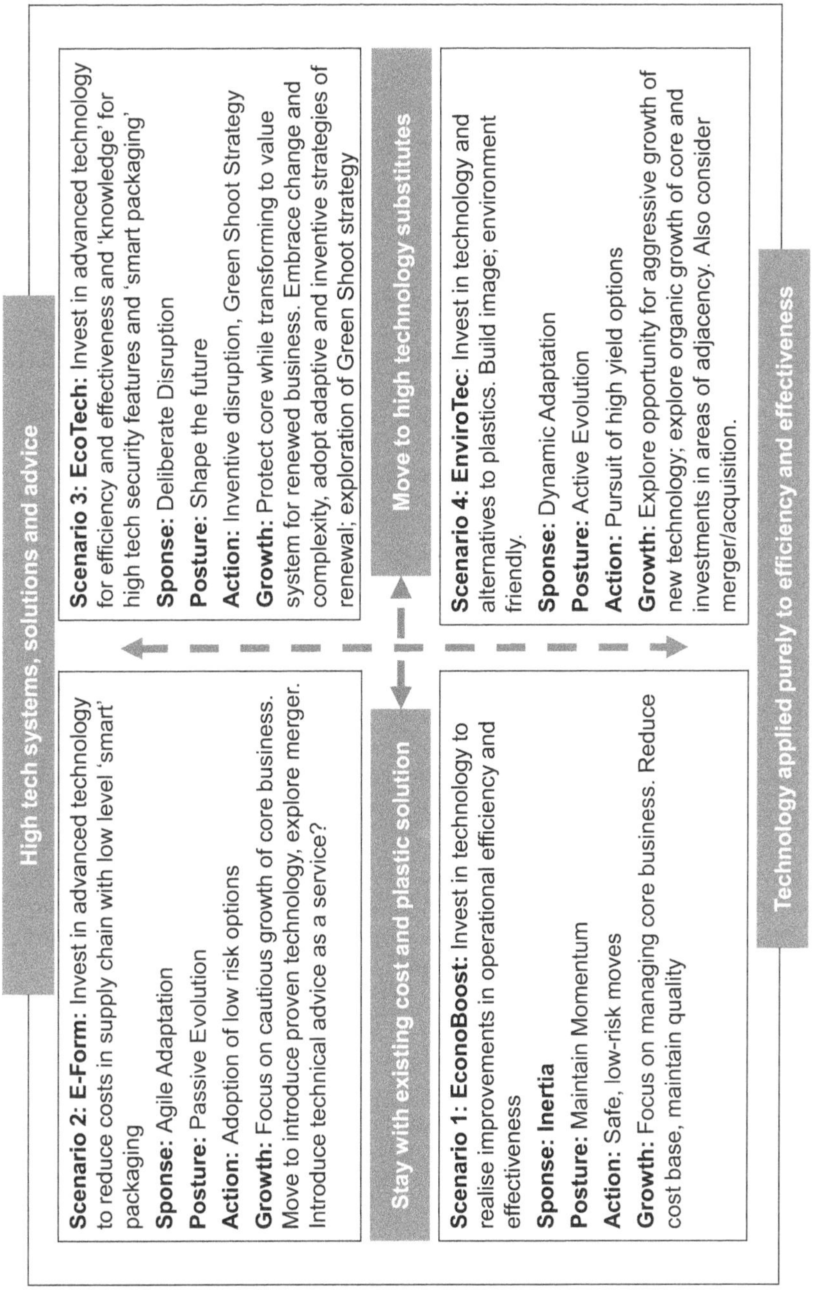
High tech systems, solutions and advice
Scenario 2: E-Form: Invest in advanced technology to reduce costs in supply chain with low level 'smart' packaging
Sponse: Agile Adaptation
Posture: Passive Evolution
Action: Adoption of low risk options
Growth: Focus on cautious growth of core business. Move to introduce proven technology, explore merger. Introduce technical advice as a service?
Scenario 3: EcoTech: Invest in advanced technology for efficiency and effectiveness and 'knowledge' for high tech security features and 'smart packaging'
Sponse: Deliberate Disruption
Posture: Shape the future
Action: Inventive disruption, Green Shoot Strategy
Growth: Protect core while transforming to value system for renewed business. Embrace change and complexity, adopt adaptive and inventive strategies of renewal; exploration of Green Shoot strategy
Stay with existing cost and plastic solution
Move to high technology substitutes
Scenario 1: EconoBoost: Invest in technology to realise improvements in operational efficiency and effectiveness
Sponse: Inertia
Posture: Maintain Momentum
Action: Safe, low-risk moves
Growth: Focus on managing core business. Reduce cost base, maintain quality
Scenario 4: EnviroTec: Invest in technology and alternatives to plastics. Build image; environment friendly.
Sponse: Dynamic Adaptation
Posture: Active Evolution
Action: Pursuit of high yield options
Growth: Explore opportunity for aggressive growth of new technology; explore organic growth of core and investments in areas of adjacency. Also consider merger/acquisition.
Technology applied purely to efficiency and effectiveness

Figure 2.8 Revised scenarios of T-wI, SPPD to include aspects of sponse and strategic postures

In seeking support of this idea, they were buoyed by the fact that it remained consistent with their statement of Purpose, was compliant with their Mission and led them closer to their Vision. The program they chose was to seek to reinvigorate growth in core and emerging business through a philosophy of sponsive change. For the purpose of reestablishing themselves as a dominant force, they recognised the need to adopt a back-to-basics approach to strengthen core business as the first priority. While doing that, though, the leadership team also elected to explore investments in areas that they determined were reasonably lucrative advances in areas of emerging business.

To get to their desired outcomes, and for the short term at least, the leadership team accepted that they would have to plot a pathway to the future via two different avenues. The first relied on an adaptation to the reality of today. The second proposed a pathway that would lead them towards a reinvention of their envisaged future. Accordingly, they proposed to adopt an ambidextrous approach to a program that they referred to as a pathway to the future.

The ambidextrous organisation: structuring for transformation at SPPD

An ambidextrous organisation is one that is able to build new business entities out of, or as an extension of, core business. Just how to evolve a new business out of the core at low risk has always been a venture beset with difficulty and overwhelming uncertainty. Recognising the need to be more concise about the means to physically effect a transformation to a new business, Chakravarthy and Lorange (2008) provide compelling insight. In addressing the central tenet of their research question, they sought to understand

> *how does an organisation nurture core business while transforming to a new business if it is to ensure a sustainable and profitable future?*

The best solution, they observed, was the establishment of an ambidextrous transformational program. As illustrated in Figure 2.9, Jenny and Alicia adapted Chakravarthy and Lorange's (2008) solution to evolve a matrix that depicts a 'pathway to growth' that they could apply to SPPD.

Taking the option of both an Inside Out and Outside In approach to strategy, Jenny and Alicia applied the dimensions of distinctive competences and renewable markets to the ambidextrous transformation matrix demonstrated in Figure 2.9. Their starting point was the bottom-left quartile that represents existing competences and existing markets or, in other words, core business. The strategy adopted by participants in this quartile is to nurture and optimise the existing business opportunities. It is the extension of this component of the business that is being addressed overall. Characteristics of each quartile are described as follows:

- **Leverage:** Pursuit of opportunities identified in new markets obtained by building and leveraging existing competences

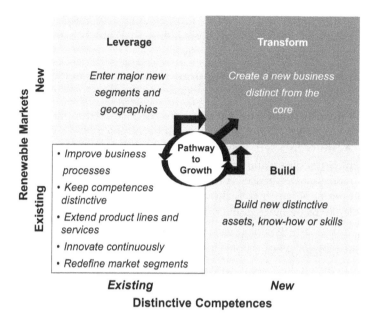

Figure 2.9 Illustrative progress of ambidextrous organisation: building from the core, transformation and renewal to the business of the future

- **Build:** Extension of presence in existing markets through deployment of new competences, resources and assets
- **Transform:** Entry into new markets that require new competences (and maybe a Core Competence Platform) evolved from a strength in existing resources. The objective here is to create a new business altogether, noting that its roots can be found very firmly in the firm's core business

Ambidextrous pathways to implementation at SPPD

Ambidextrousness in the context of the challenge facing SPPD refers to its ability to conduct two programs of performance improvement at the same time. The two proposed pathways were described by the leadership team and communicated to the organisation through a series of presentations and 'town hall' meetings. The ambidextrous transformation program to be adopted by SPPD is described in the context of two (new) pathways:

Pathway 1: Agile Adaptation: Nurture and optimise core business:

- **Posture: passive evolution:** Evaluate options as a follower of change

- **Action: adoption of options:** Decisions that yield signifcant posi-tive payoffs: Initial cautious growth subject to cash constraints and executive capabilities steadily building to a state of rapid transforma-tion in alignment with Pathway 2

Pathway 2: Deliberate Disruption: Transform to a multidextrous, Inte-gratedValue System service provider:

- **Posture: shape the future:** Take the lead in the pursuit of multi-opportunities with the objective of becoming a Hyper – HPO
- **Action: focused organisational transformation and renewal:** Exploration of, and initially cautious investment in, evolutionary but rapid transformation. Although the pursuit of Green Shoot Strategy options (Chapter 6) is also a possibility, this activity was considered by Jenny to be more distractive then helpful at this stage of the transfor-mation journey

In its implementation,Alicia and Jenny gladly adopted the ambidextrous organ-isation structuring doctrine (Chakravarthy and Lorange, 2008) that suggested,

SPPD should establish separate project teams that were structurally inde-pendent from each pathway but were also integrated into the existing man-agement hierarchy.

An illustration of this structure is shown as Figure 2.10.

Rather excitingly, they thought a reinvention of their entire business was in order. Electing to adopt an IntegratedValue Systems perspective, they thought that rather than selling individual products and services alone, they could com-bine each to form a systems–based and fully integrated service offering. Such

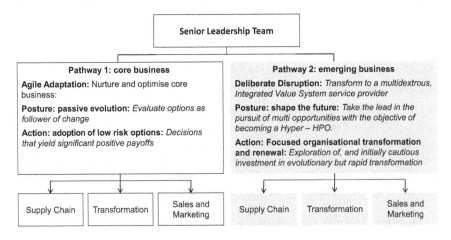

Figure 2.10 Illustrative structuring of ambidextrous organisational transformation

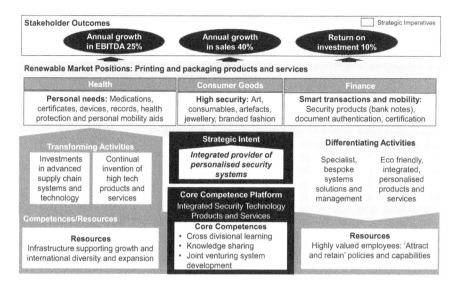

Figure 2.11 A newly revised Strategic Architecture for SPPD

a solution would lead to greater efficiency and effectiveness in supply, as well as greater value to its customers and a greater opportunity to build and retain their trust and loyalty. At this stage, however, they weren't sure what that would look like. Similarly, they recognised the benefits of creating a Core Competence Platform, but they were unsure what that would look like either. They decided, therefore, to start with a rough idea and monitor closely to see how well it would work in practice. An illustrative Strategic Architecture depicting this third iteration of Long Term Strategy was considered. With a Strategic Intent of "integrated provider of personalised security systems", their objective now was to

reflect an identity for SPPD that would incorporate their ambition to transition to a high-technology and Integrated Value System service provider.

Fundamental to the message of personalisation was the division of their market representation into three customer-focused divisions: health, consumer goods and finance. They also sought to include in this revised Strategic Architecture their existing notion of what a Core Competence Platform could be. Although they were in the early days, Alicia was satisfied that it would be an integral component of their ongoing transformation journey. A newly revised Strategic Architecture for this revised focus appears in Figure 2.11.

The reinvention of SPPD into that service provider is explored further in the next chapter (Chapter 3).

3 Reinventing Strategic Planning

Chapter overview

Contemporary strategy practice is traditionally conducted through the use of a mixed bag of tools and techniques. It has been hard to bind these into a common form and format for the purpose of conducting a clear and concise evaluation of strategic options. In this chapter, we find a solution to this dilemma. This is realised through the application of systems thinking and Flood's (1999) notion of systemic evaluation, shaping (*methods deployed*) and reviewing (*lessons learned*).

Strategy Evaluation is a methodology deployed to both formulate strategy and review its effectiveness post-implementation. In our exploration of Strategy Evaluation, Shaping, practitioners are advised to consider the need for a degree of deep, critical, strategic thinking; the application of open strategy practice; and its conduct within a context of a Community of Strategy Practice. Rather than forming a strategic plan, however, it is recommended practitioners instead seek to evolve an ongoing Strategy Narrative as a basis upon which assessments of strategic options are explored and a Strategy Blueprint is developed.

In our exploration of Strategy Evaluation, Reviewing, we introduce the mechanism that assesses the effectiveness of strategy. Its application to practice is primarily affected and discussed through the operation and management of a Program of Continual Strategy Renewal (Chapter 4).

Learning insights

Strategy is about the future, but the future is difficult to accurately predict. There is a need, therefore, to draw on as much information as possible to make informed decisions about what should be done in the short term if the organisation is going to realise its Purpose, Mission, Vision in the long term. A lack of certainty, however, means that many of the predictions and decisions made will be based on the less certain foundation of gut feelings, assumptions, estimates and guesstimates in the strategy formulation process. There is a need, therefore, to enact a process of Strategy Evaluation, Reviewing in order to follow up on gut feelings–based assumptions, as there is a considerably high probability that they will be wrong as often as they are right.

The concept of Strategy Evaluation, Shaping, particularly in the form of strategy formulation tools and techniques, has long been a focus for academics and non-academics alike. It is useful therefore to explore, define and explain some of the more common tools in this chapter and their categorisation in the form of a strategy toolbox. Recognising the propensity for error in the use of predictions and assumptions, however, it is also useful to explore some of the human elements that can both enhance our strategy-making ability and impede it. Examples of the former are the use of deep critical thinking, design thinking and value of open strategy practice conducted in the environment of a Community of Strategy Practice. An example of the latter is the existence of bias as a key contributor to the downside of the use of an open strategy practice.

In our application of these methodologies to SPPD, it is helpful to demonstrate not only their use in practice but also how important and inevitable a need to evaluate and re-evaluate strategic decision making is, especially when establishing an internal strategic management capability from scratch.

Work plan phase 3: reinventing Strategic Planning: Strategy Evaluation

Explored in this chapter is content depicted in the third phase of the project work plan presented in Table 3.1. Addressing the concept of Strategy Evaluation in the context of a reinvention of Strategic Planning, the primary topics to be reviewed are Strategy Evaluation, Shaping and Reviewing, the notion of a Strategy Narrative, the conduct of deep strategic thinking and the establishment of a Strategy Blueprint.

Introduction: the notion of Strategy Evaluation

We apply a systems-based approach to evaluation, which in the context of strategy enables us to "achieve a balance between instrumental action (methods deployed) and experiential action (lessons learned)" (Flood, 1999). In our adaptation of the notion of evaluation, we refer to Flood's naming of *methods deployed* as Strategy Evaluation, Shaping and *lessons learned* as Strategy Evaluation,

Table 3.1 Steps/dates: development and delivery of a strategy and leadership development program at client organisation: Phase 3

Phase 3: Strategy Evaluation	Chapter 3
1 **Conduct analysis:** Strategy Evaluation Shaping and incubator workshop(s)	
2 **Form consensus:** Final Strategic Architecture, Strategy Narrative, draft Strategy Blueprint, Strategy Evaluation, Reviewing program	
3 **Establish support network:** Internal change management agency, 'Community of Strategy Practice' (COSP), foundation of formal organisation learning facility	
4 **Design:** Strategy Evaluation, Reviewing network and infrastructure	
5 **Confirm next steps:** Follow Program of Continual Strategy Renewal	

Reviewing. As the key component of the second element of the framework, our purpose in the use of Systemic Strategy Evaluation activities is to

*   provide content for the formulation of Long and Short Term Strategy and shape the way it is implemented;
*   supply the means for reviewing the effectiveness of outputs from strategy and the systems, processes and methods deployed to derive, develop and update strategy; and
*   contribute informed content of importance to strategy, ideally in conjunction with a formal organisational learning capability.

Definitions of Strategy Evaluation, Shaping and Strategy Evaluation, Reviewing are described as follows:

*   **Strategy Evaluation, Shaping:** Evaluation through instrumental action (methods deployed). An evaluation of outcomes from tools and techniques (e.g. scenario analysis, market share analysis) that contribute to an update of Long Term Strategy and/or informs the short term Strategy Narrative and subsequent Strategy Blueprint.
*   **Strategy Evaluation, Reviewing:** Evaluation through experiential action (lessons learned). Essentially an evaluation of the effectiveness of the outputs from, and effectiveness of, strategy and its capacity to inform the strategic decision-making process. This includes an specific systems, processes and methods deployed to update and develop strategy that is both long and short term in perspective . It also includes an organisational learning capability that incorporates a capacity to capture lessons learned from both Strategy Evaluation, Shaping and Reviewing activities.

An illustration of the Strategy Evaluation micro-system is shown as a form of reinvention of the process of Strategic Planning in Figure 3.1.

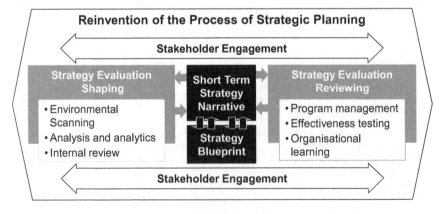

Figure 3.1 Systemic Strategy Evaluation micro-system and the role of a Strategy Narrative as the foundation for the Strategy Blueprint

Redefining Long Term Strategy at T-wI, SPPD

T-wI, SPPD has always been an Inside Out–oriented business. For years, it has successfully leveraged its many patented, specialist and, quite often, inimitable resources into its chosen markets. The last thing that Division Managing Director Jenny Wong felt she should do, therefore, was to destroy or, worse still, outsource those essential customer-focused resources through a short term, broad-based cost-reduction program. She did need to make them more efficient and effective in the short term, but that was what she was good at.

Her concern now, therefore, was to ensure that she and her executive team could turn their attention to all of the aspects of the content reflected in their recently completed Strategic Architecture (Figure 2.11). The fact that it could operate as an Inside Out– and Outside In–oriented system was quite a revelation to her and the team. Although improvements in short term operating performance were critical, long term growth, she now recognised, would be dependent on establishing a much stronger presence in the marketplace. Fundamental to that objective was her recognition that a reorientation to an Outside In market focus would also require a corresponding transformation in the resources SPPD would require to service those markets. The combined effect, she realised, would mean that instead of promoting and selling the goods and services SPPD liked to make, they would now need to identify the goods and services they would *have* to make to meet the demands of the industries, markets and customers that represented the greatest opportunity for financial and social return.

Apart from any of the other pressing issues SPPD faced, Jenny recognised that SPPD had reached a tipping point that would require a change in focus and thereby a change in structure. The tipping point she had reached was similar to one that all chocolate manufacturers had reached on their journey of ongoing transformation and renewal from producers of raw cacao seeds to that of suppliers of smooth milk chocolate confectionery and chocolate bars. The story of the transformation of the chocolate industry from investigative researchers and development specialists to market gurus is described in Case example 3.1. It is the story of the evolution of the chocolate manufacturers Nestlé, Cadbury and Hershey that commenced in the mid-1800s. It also includes the relative newcomer to the industry, Mars Inc., that was not established until 1911.

Case example 3.1: A gradual transformation from Inside Out to Outside In, reaching a point of strategic equilibrium within the global chocolate confectionery industry

Global chocolate manufacturers Nestlé, Cadbury, Mars and Hershey evolved from humble origins. Each were independent pioneers in the art of chocolate manufacture which saw them evolve a bitter-tasting cacao seed into a chocolate drink and then smooth sweet tasting chocolate bars.

Inside Out origins

In order to reach the point of chocolate Utopia each of these manufacturers had to endure an extensive period (around 100 years) of focused research and development from the 1830s, in Cadbury's case, until the early 1900s (Cadbury, 2010). Throughout this period, they undertook relentless laboratory research and trialling of recipes and production processes in their mission to transform the humble cacao seed into a high volume and delectable milk chocolate product. Carrying an inherent bitter flavour, the first challenge set for the scientists was to turn raw cacao seed into a reasonable tasting chocolate drink. Its transformation into a solid chocolate bar, however, wouldn't be perfected until the researchers were able to blend the cacao seed with milk at the turn of the century. This was not an easy task given the fact that the solid fatty content of the raw cacao seed was difficult to mix with the milk liquid.

An Inside Out revolution

The breakthroughs didn't all occur at the same time. Cadbury, for example, was some ten years behind its competitors in the development of its Cadbury Dairy Milk product (Cadbury, 2010). Similarly, not all manufacturers followed the same recipe. Differentiation in taste between each manufacturer was quite noticeable and strategically important. As a rule, consumers will always retain a preference for the first brand of chocolate they taste, making it a good way to retain customer loyalty at the least.

As a result of the breakthrough, chocolate manufacturers invested in large-scale manufacturing production lines and started turning out chocolate bars by the tonne. Once high-volume production was mastered, the product became so popular, its consumption escalated to that of a high-volume commodity. Other than the difference in flavours, differentiation and, therefore, growth in market share was quite problematic

An Outside In revolution

The chocolate industry was booming in the early part of the 1900s. The Great Depression, two world wars, random revolutions and an abundance of other economic interruptions made life difficult for chocolate producers. The real pressure from competition, however, arrived in the mid-1960s. During a period of post-war growth and prosperity, the arrival of the supermarket in the 1960s saw a revolution in the way food was sold to consumers. Cadbury, for example, was the owner of the corner store–styled customer for mass-produced chocolate blocks (Cadbury, 2010). Mars, on the other hand, had been nurturing the emerging supermarket industry for a while. It was the winner in the industry transformation to supermarket trade and the market for confectionery-oriented chocolate bars, such as the Mars Bar and Milky Way, each an attractive alternative to plain chocolate bars. Cadbury, on the other hand, faltered as its capital intensive and inflexible production plant was no match for the agile Mars and its lean distribution network.

By the time the late 1900s had arrived, chocolate had become a commodity-oriented and highly competitive product. Manufacturers found that they needed to amass a large market share if they were to survive.

The transformation from Inside Out to Outside In was well underway

Chocolate confectionery producers would now need to find points of differentiation in their marketing as opposed to the markets *per se*. In addition to the arrival of low-cost, efficient supermarkets free to air television advertising, and lower prices for the chocolate product overall made for a much broader product reach. Each manufacturer was forced to fight harder for market share. All sought to benefit from their own points of differentiation, none of which were overly compelling. At the same time, chocolate became an obvious target for the discounted supermarket home brand lines.

The maturation bubble

By the time the end of the 20th century had arrived, nearly every chocolate manufacture had arrived at the same point of strategic equilibrium (Figure 3.2) shown on the SMI Model of Equilibrium indicator. Most manufacturers had outsourced the majority of their chocolate base production facilities to specialist manufacturers. Their only points of differentiation had become their brand names (Nestlé, Mars, Cadbury, Hershey) and, accordingly, the colour of their packaging, the shape of their chocolate bars, their generally unique flavours, the form of their products (caramel and other fillings vs. plain chocolate) and their price.

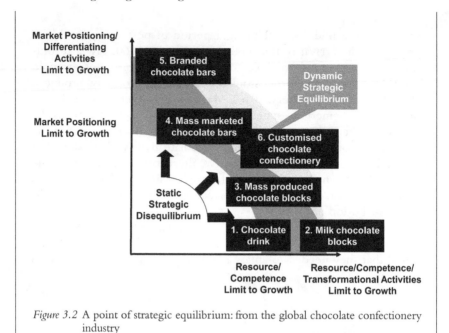

Figure 3.2 A point of strategic equilibrium: from the global chocolate confectionery industry

SPPD was in a very similar situation to these pioneering chocolate manufacturers. Jenny saw that and was keen to take control of the inevitable transformation that would take place in SPPD's business environment.

Strategy Evaluation, Shaping: enabling structured and unstructured strategic thinking

Although not yet formalised in SPPD, the leadership team had already learned and appreciated a lot more about the future and its potential through their engagement in the SPPD scenario analysis exercises, as depicted in Figure 2.9. To help her evaluate and understand their options for market alternatives, Alicia encouraged her colleagues to embark on a new program of Strategy Evaluation, Shaping. The process of Strategy Evaluation, Shaping differentiates between the two external environment categories and the internal environment, as illustrated in Figure 3.3.

The SPPD leadership team had done a pretty good job of analysing the impact that the Level 1 external environment would have on their business through the conduct of the PESTE analysis and associated scenario analysis that were explored in Chapters 1 and 2. Alicia had advised Jenny, however, that there was still more structured and unstructured forms of analysis that they could do at Levels 1, 2 and 3. At Level 1, Alicia advised Jenny that in addition to the PESTE and scenario analysis, she had found the Five Forces analysis to have provided useful insight, at least as a one-off analytical tool. She also proposed the use of 'backcasting' to provide insight into the development of expectations

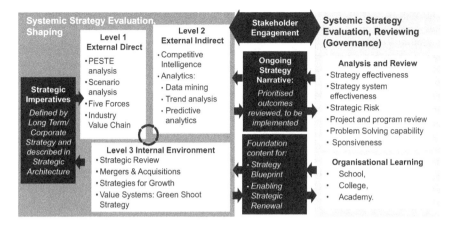

Figure 3.3 Systemic Strategy Evaluation and a Strategy Narrative as the foundation for the Strategy Blueprint

for the implementation journey. Jenny encouraged Alicia, therefore, to work with the leadership team to develop each of those models further. At Level 2, Alicia sought to establish a strategy education program and an associated strategy toolkit in order to consolidate and evolve their capacity for structured strategic analysis. At Level 3, Alicia sought to explore the application of alternative forms of strategic thinking to their strategy practitioner's skill base. Analytical tools and approaches to strategic thinking found points of differentiation between structured and unstructured analysis.

Level 1: Outside In, external indirect: models enabling structured strategic thinking

Alicia commenced her review at this level with the execution of a Five Forces analysis (Porter, 1980). Competitiveness is the primary objective of strategy according to Porter (1980), author of the Five Forces model. His model is designed specifically to provide insight into the attractiveness of an investment in any one industry. As a rule, Porter (1980) observed, "an 'attractive' industry is one in which the combination of these five forces acts to drive up overall profitability". An unattractive industry does the opposite, however: "A very unattractive industry is one which is approaching 'pure competition' in which case available profits for all firms are driven down to zero". It is true that the overall industry attractiveness does not imply that every firm in the industry will return the same levels of profitability. It is also true that in the context of Third Wave Strategy, a clear and concise definition of 'industry' will be difficult to establish. It's clear, for example, which industry the Amazon online bookstore entered when it was established. As a provider of e-commerce, cloud computing, digital streaming and artificial intelligence, a definition of the industry in which Amazon operates is a little harder to define. The same applies to Ford – as it earnestly seeks to traverse a number of industry boundaries in its endeavour to become a mobility company as opposed to a manufacturer operating in the automotive industry.

Alicia chose to select a broad interpretation of the definition of industry in her application of the Five Forces model to SPPD. The result of her analysis appears in Table 3.2. Jenny found the knowledge gleaned from the Five Forces analysis to be useful, especially given her objective of becoming a more Outside In–focused business. That was, after all, what Pathway 1: Agile Adaptation: Nurture and optimise core business was all about. As far as Pathway 2: Deliberate Disruption: Transform to a multidextrous, Integrated Value System service provider was concerned, however, Jenny felt more work needed to be done. In particular, Jenny felt the Five Forces model was of greater help to those following a strategy of industry followership as opposed to industry leadership.

Either way, the proposed journey of transformation was a big and extremely important program. Alicia sought to apply another technique she had used in her role as a management consultant prior to its implementation in order to get a better handle on the dimensions of the journey proposed. It was the adoption of a program referred to as backcasting. As a concept, it is literally the opposite of forecasting. To illustrate its application to SPPD, Alicia asked Jenny to work with the leadership team to track the journey that they supposed would get them to their ideas of SPPD some 20 to 50 years hence.

Armed with shared insight from their preferred scenario, their natural reaction had been to envisage the current format of the company and fast forward to the associated images 20 or more years into the future. As Alicia delighted in pointing out, however, it was obvious that their versions of the journey to the future would likely be clouded by embedded mental models depicting perceptions of a transformation journey based on *what is*. The risk in this, she observed, was that natural biases would strongly influence their thinking towards perceptions of the journey they would 'like to take' but not necessarily an optimal journey that they 'could or should take'. As an alternative, Alicia next asked them to start their thinking at the time that the scenarios depict, some 20 years hence and work back to today. Illustrated in Figure 3.4, the value of backcasting lies in the fact that the closer you get from your virtual perception of the future, the more insight about the reality of the journey you would take today. You end up not only with a much clearer picture of a collective view of the future but also imagined aspects of the journey that you will have to negotiate along the way.

Level 2: Outside In, external, direct: models of structured and unstructured strategic thinking

In addition to the tools and techniques used to enable structured strategic thinking at Level 1, Alicia had spent some time learning about the aspects of unstructured strategic thinking that could both enhance and encumber healthy strategic decision making at SPPD at Level 2. There was, of course, no one tool, technique or characteristic of structured strategic thinking that would provide the level of insight and foresight that she considered essential to SPPD's future needs.

Table 3.2 Porter's Five Forces analysis of relevance to SPPD

Threat of suppliers: Bargaining power of suppliers **Conclusion: Strong** influence, difficult to find specialists in their industry	SPPD suppliers extract a premium from SPPD. Other than high-volume plastic substrate for its packaging division, SPPD tended to procure only small volumes of their suppliers' outputs relative to the end product manufactured by them. Examples are plastic and metal componentry, holograms, RFID, other electronic componentry and other forms of microchips. Their suppliers, therefore, could exist without them but would miss the extra volume they could get from SPPD at a premium price. Because there aren't many suppliers, it was more in SPPD's interest to ensure that they remained viable rather than obtaining the lowest price. SPPD couldn't operate without them and switching suppliers would be difficult.
Threat of potential entrants: Threat of new entrants **Conclusion:** Threat is high in commodity products and low but under threat in speciality products	New digital technology developers represent a fearsome and unknown threat to SPPD which operates in a quite specialised field with a finite number of potential new customers in its current markets. There is little obvious threat from new entrants; however, the opportunity is there for that to occur, and they have already lost more new business than they would like over time. What Alicia, Jenny and the SPPD team were most afraid of was the unknown more than the known. As a result of the massive rise in digital technology, new competitors could emerge from anywhere, at any time. Equally, Alicia was constantly on the lookout for new opportunities for SPPD to build on its resource base and to leverage that into new markets and new industries altogether.
Threat of industry competitors: Rivalry amongst existing firms **Conclusion:** Same situation as threat of new entrants	Globally, there are only a few competitors in this industry in most of SPPD markets. It operates in a relatively unique and specialist field which enjoys a cost advantage because of higher volume sales than most of its competitors. Specific security features for passports, for example, are different for each country. Overall, competition isn't as much a part of SPPD's life, therefore, as it would be for those participants in the automotive or supermarket industries, for example. Cost competitiveness also varies by product category. Packaging is most profitable when it can obtain economies of scale and, therefore, lower operating costs through long-run, high-volume production. Printing and other speciality products suffer from the burden of short-run batches, but because of their extensive industry experience, SPPD is able to contain costs, keeping their exposure to competitive pricing to a minimum. There is an imperative, however, for SPPD to regain the lead in technology development as there are many start-ups already appearing on the horizon. Each have the potential to gain business from SPPD.

(Continued)

Table 3.2 (Continued)

Threat of buyers: Bargaining power of buyers **Conclusion:** High as opportunities for substitute products increase	SPPD's biggest weakness lies in this area because of its longevity. SPPD has more ownership over its customers than competitors, for now. Their level of power, however, has faded somewhat in recent times, as its momentum has dwindled over the years. There is no reason why they could not regain market share if they can get more reliability and momentum into their customer service capabilities. To survive long term, it has to find a way to transform, renew and find a way to deliver a much greater 'value proposition' to its customers than it is today.
Substitutes: Threat of substitutes **Conclusion:** Emerging threats but on the whole not high – for now	An emerging phenomenon as new technology and the possibility of new kinds of security features evolve. In core business areas, there are few threats, as SPPD's purpose in life is to prevent duplication and forging, copying or imitating of any kind.
Complementors: Threat of complementors **Conclusion:** High for any potential complementor but at the same time high for SPPD to do the same thing	A recent and sixth addition to the Five Forces model. The potential to define service offerings from complementarity are significant, as is the opportunity for others to incorporate security features into their own Integrated Value System. Complementarity, therefore, is a significant point of interest for Alicia and Jenny. SPPD has long lamented the fact that much of their effectiveness relies on the capacity of a machine to read the signals or readings that are emitted from their proprietary technology, for example. Similarly, their service offering is only partly applied to their product offering and, thereby, their customers' total level of expenditure in this key area of their business.

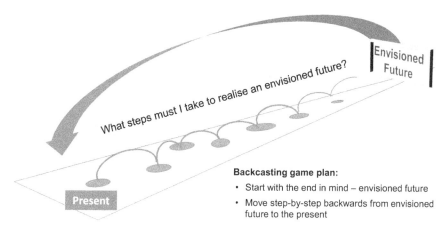

Figure 3.4 Backcasting an envisioned future

Rather, she noted, it would be useful to provide an agglomeration of the various tools, activities, exercises and approaches to strategic thinking that would then lead to a greater capability in strategy overall. Accordingly, she had gone to some lengths to set up an education program that would help others to better understand how they could be best managed and applied to SPPD's specific needs.

The strategy education program she devised was oriented towards that of business acumen and leadership development rather than that of strategy *per se*. The purpose of her coursework was to provide the means by which participants could structure their strategic thinking while at the same time exercise an assessment and judgement of the outcomes from practical strategising activities. The value of their contribution could be seen in the formation and implementation of strategic decisions and, thereby, better strategy content. Based on the construct of the Third Wave Strategy framework, the primary objective of the Strategy Evaluation, Shaping program Alicia designed sought to provide input to a short term Strategy Narrative. As part of a system, its purpose was also to provide insight into the continued relevance of SPPD Long Term Strategy. In order to make sure this and other strategic programs were implemented effectively, Alicia now thought it was time seek permission to a find and appoint a senior executive who would assume responsibility for the management and implementation of this program. Jenny agreed and Alicia was was delighted to offer the position to a former colleague, Charles Bakersfield. Charles was only too pleased to accept. His title would be Executive General Manager, Strategy and Transformation.

Structured strategic thinking

Fundamental to effectiveness of structured strategic thinking is access to strategy tools and techniques and an education program in how to use them. A starting

Table 3.3 Strategy toolkit enabling structured strategic thinking

Strategy **tool**	Description of strategy tool
Level 1: Outside In, external indirect: universally focused environmental scanning	
Political, economic, social, technological and ecological (PESTE) analysis	An examination of the midterm (10–15 years) from PESTE dimensions.
Five Forces analysis	Identifies those econometrically focused 'forces' that contribute to competitive intensity in an industry and thereby the attractiveness of an investment in that industry (Porter, 1985).
Scenario analysis	Provide conceptual insight into 'imagined' perspectives of the future that represent issues of complexity and uncertainty as they provide insight into a distinctly possible and plausible (but not necessarily probable) worlds (Wack, 1985).
Level 2: Outside In, external, direct environment: industry- and market-level orientation	
Game theory	Game theory relates to a set of concepts aimed at decision making in situations of competition and conflict, as well as cooperation and interdependence. Can be applied in situations where two or more participants are faced with choices of action, by which each may gain or lose, depending on what others choose to do or not to do. Provides many insights into the behaviour of oligopolists (Nalebuff and Brandenburger, 1995).
Business model	Constructed in two parts, a business model "Incorporates all the activities associated with making something: designing it, purchasing raw materials, manufacturing, and so on", and second, "Identifies and describes all the activities a company does to sell their goods or services". These include finding and reaching customers, transacting a sale, distributing the product or delivering the service (Magretta, 2002).
Value chain	Describes the structure of activities that are undertaken to transform organisational resources into goods and services and as an outcome, profit. The value chain categorises the generic value-adding activities of an organisation. They are differentiated between direct activities (examples are design, production and delivery of goods and services) and indirect support activities (examples are accounting, human resources, sales and marketing) (Porter, 1985).
Industry value chain	Identifying opportunities to share resources, capabilities and management systems across multiple businesses (Porter, 1985).

Competitive intelligence	Interactive competitor and industry-/arena-/domain-specific data monitoring mechanism maintained as an embedded (intranet portal) program that monitors strategies and activities of competitors and potential competitors (Calof and Wright, 2008).
The three horizons model	Provides insight into a variety of alternative futures – a focus on building and maintaining the pipeline (Baghai et al., 1999).
Ansoff product/market matrix	The Ansoff Product-Market Growth Matrix allows strategists to consider ways to grow the business via existing and/or new products and existing and/or new markets (Ansoff, 1957).
BCG and McKinsey market share matrices	The initial intent of the potential growth-share matrix was to evaluate business units. Subsequent versions allowed for product lines or any other cash-generating entities to be assessed (Hedley, 1977).
Blue Ocean Strategy	Blue Ocean Strategy is used to determine where high growth and profits can be generated through the creation of new demand in an uncontested market space, or a 'Blue Ocean', instead of by competing head-to-head with other suppliers for known customers in an existing industry 'Red Ocean' (Kim and Mauborgne, 2005).
Multidimensional scaling	Illustrative maps of consumer perceptions of competing products along key differentiating variables (Grant, 2016).
Conjunct analysis	Uses estimates of consumer preferences for particular product attributes to forecast demand for new products that comprise different bundles of product attributes (Grant, 2016).
Hedonic price analysis	Estimates of the price that consumers will pay for particular product attributes (Grant, 2016).

Level 3: Inside Out, internal environment: resource and core competence orientation

Activity-based cost analysis	Traditionally a cost-management tool that enables more concise allocation of costs to systems, processes, goods and services. Can be used to redefine resources but also assess the effectiveness of resource allocation and strategy profiles, especially in the context of the SMI Model of Dynamic Strategic Equilibrium (Kaplan and Anderson, 2004).
Core competence analysis	Capacity for learning in the organisation, especially how to coordinate diverse production skills and integrate multiple streams of technology (Prahalad and Hamel, 1990).

Third Wave Strategy: addressing complex strategic problems

Strategic Architecture, Strategy Blueprint and SMI Model of Strategic Equilibrium	An overview of all content of relevance to a firm-specific, long term Strategic Architecture and short term Strategy Blueprint. Along with the outcome of deep strategic thinking, these constructs also provide insight into gaps in strategy, causality/alignment between Inside Out and Outside In and the basis for equilibrium.
Strategic business intelligence	Technologically, mostly digital sources data of significance to the strategic future of the business.

point for content to be included in the strategy toolkit is presented in Table 3.3. The education program that Alicia had already started with Charles Bakersfield was a natural home for this program.

Level 3: Inside Out, internal environment: unstructured strategic thinking

Fundamental to the effectiveness of Inside Out, unstructured strategic thinking is an ability to understand what it is. A summary of some common approaches to unstructured strategic thinking follow. These too, Alicia thought, should be incorporated into an SPPD formal education program.

Design thinking

One-time CEO of the idea invention company IDEO, Tim Brown (2008), described design thinking as

> *a discipline that uses a designer's sensibility and methods to match people's needs with what is technologically feasible and what a viable business strategy can convert into customer value and market opportunity.*

The IDEO website today describes design thinking as simply "a process for creative problem solving", and so it is. Although design thinking is often considered to be an unstructured form of strategic thinking, Brown (2008) provided some procedural steps that provide guidance to its implementation.

As with any problem–solving methodology, the first step is to fully understand what the problem is – a task that is not always that easy to do. As an example, it is generally known that abnormal flooding, forest fires and snowfall patterns have been creating havoc and hardship in many people's lives this century. While many administrators are calling for better fire, flood and snow management to solve the problem, however, others are calling for better management of the earth's entire climate. Those in the former camp define the problem as an environmental hazard. Those in the latter define it as a global ecological emergency.

We adapt the Brown (2008) design thinking methodology to explore ways to reach resolution of difficult strategic problems. His first step is to evoke a spirit of inspiration.

1   **Inspiration:** In evoking inspiration, Brown is encouraging the problem resolution group to engage, explore and confirm the exact nature and basis of the problem and what added value or enhancement they can bring to its resolution. In our natural disaster example, the problem can be seen to be much more than abnormal events. Should it be interpreted to be an issue of global climate change, certain individuals will be highly inspired to be given the opportunity to find solutions to this high-profile, and apparently devastating, issue. Others may be more inclined to look at the problem of forest fires, for example, as a cause of human lung disease and, accordingly,

be inspired to find a solution to that. Others may be inspired simply by being asked to solve the problem of out of control forest fires. It is necessary to confirm, therefore, what the real problem is that the design thinking mechanism is trying to address and why.

In doing so, Brown (2018) encouraged the researchers to dig deep, share their thoughts through open discussion and use tools such as full- or short-form scenario analysis, sketches, Lego brick simulations or storytelling. The application of reframing would also be applicable here, as would systems thinking, perhaps in a context of organisational learning.

2   **Ideation:** Once opportunities for problem resolution have been identified, it is then a good idea, according to Brown (2008), to confirm what the priorities are in association with the identification of what needs to be done. This is where the real design component of design thinking comes into play. Brown (2018) encouraged the use of brainstorming sessions that deploy sketches, scenarios and other stakeholder insights as input to resolution development. The solutions shortlisted for implementation should then be tested and, where appropriate, prototypes developed to reflect the solution in practice. This, he suggested, should be an iterative process that entails the testing and retesting of proposed alternative solutions. Feedback should also be sought from a broad range of contributors. Once the solution has been evolved, the final step is its implementation.

3   **Implementation:** This is a straightforward exercise that is consistent with our concept of a Program of Continual Strategy Renewal. Brown (2008) suggested it is not a good idea to simply apply a 'set and forget' measure but to instead engage in several rounds of 'trial and error' to ensure that the final solution is the optimal one.

Systemic Cognitive Strategy Practice: fortuitive strategic thinking

As a non-structured and often 'sticky', complex and incomprehensible topic laced with wicked strategic problems, Third Wave Strategy Evaluation, Shaping activities also recognise the need to apply deep, focused, intuitive and future-oriented strategic thinking. We refer to this as *fortuitive* strategic thinking. This, This form of thinking, is conducted by a specialist group of talented and committed individuals in a format that we refer to as Systemic Cognitive Strategy Practice (SCSP). The formation of an SCSP team represents one of the most significant departures from the notion of deliberate, static Strategic Planning as it has evolved into an emergent, systemic, dynamic practice. SCSP elevates the notion of strategy from conceptualisation of future outcomes, and attempts to pre-empt them, to that of a continual consciousness and renewal of an organisation's value creation measures and the means to implement them.

SCSP is a part of organisational learning; it is based on an analysis of intuitive judgement and decisions made in the past. It is also based on individual and group interpretations and of 1) the reality of the present combined with

2) informed fortuitive judgement, forecasts and predictions (digital analytically derived or otherwise) of the future. While the idea of open strategy practice carries with it a promise of openness, transparency, generality and accountability for all, SCSP cardholders are charged with the conduct of problem-specific, deep-dive strategic analysis. The intent is not to establish another elite SWAT team. Rather, it is to establish a group of future-focused, strategically oriented enthusiasts who are already working within or in a capacity that is closely aligned to the organisation's strategy and its future. Their knowledge may be garnered from those possessing advanced insight and a comprehensive analytical capability or those simply occupying an informed position in the firm (for example, customer service officers, holders of intellectual property or incumbents in some form of specialist role). This core SCSP group will represent a broad-based membership drawn from across the business and from outside the business when suitable. The group will potentially be brought together through their membership of a specialist 'Community of Strategy Practice' (COSP).

Community of Strategy Practice (COSP)

As discussed in Chapter 1, a COSP provides a formal and legitimate medium through which strategy can be reviewed and evaluated across a broad spectrum without any fear of recrimination or criticism. A COSP is charged with the responsibility of breaking down siloed and functional barriers; it thereby encourages cross-disciplinary discussions to take place. A COSP can be formal enough to develop policies and procedures. At the same time, it can provide the conduit to enable open and frank discussions that are strategic in nature. The COSP will not only be made up of those possessing SCSP attributes; it will also include individuals who are especially interested in the concept of strategy as an area of specialisation. These individuals will typically have the wherewithal to formally, or informally, create, invigorate, invent and enact strategic change. Holders of COSP engagement rights can be found in formal or informal positions inside and outside the business. They will be those who identify as being finely 'attuned' to the nervous system of the organisation and its stakeholders.

Individual COSP members will be informed by explicit and implicit knowledge that is found organisation wide. In the future, their knowledge will be strongly influenced and enhanced through the introduction of new knowledge-based technologies, such as cloud-based analytics, artificial intelligence and predictive/big data analytics. Everybody wins; those who are most motivated to join such a group will be those who are interested in influencing the future direction of the business. Willing participants will exist in an organisation but often in an informal capacity and in many different guises. One thing that's certain about these people is that while they will relish the opportunity to get involved and, more importantly, have their views heard, they will lose interest very quickly if their contributions are ignored.

An application of the notion of a COSP at NASA is illustrated in Case example 3.2.

Case example 3.2: Conduct of COSP at NASA

As discussed in Chapter 1 (Heracleous et al., 2019), staff members of NASA established a group that is similar in nature to a COSP. Widely recognised in NASA as the 'renegade groups', their contributions would quite often lead to the realisation of a significant strategic change. Their presence, however, was not often apparent or clear as they could be found well under the radar of any formal authority: The first – or founding member – of the NASA renegade group that subsequently transformed into a COSP nicknamed the Pirates was John Muratore, according to Heracleous et al. (2019).

Muratore was a graduate engineer who caught the attention of the leadership by diligently fixing problems wherever he came across them, even though he had not been invited to do so. To make the necessary changes to a defunct information system, for example, "Muratore connected with a small group of newly recruited engineers who felt the same way about the (the deficiencies) of that system". This group was so effective in overcoming opposition and then winning the support of high-level sponsors within NASA that it ended up "developing an entirely new shuttle mission control system", Heracleous et al. (2019) observed. Huge annualised efficiency and cost-effectiveness gains were realised as a result.

Enablers of SCSP: the concept of deep cognition

Not only are systems-based organisational learning and dialogue protocols important features of Third Wave Strategy but also the content of each needs to be relevant and appropriate. While this has to be extremely deep-seated, it will also be informed by data sourced from analytic-based business/strategic intelligence capabilities, scenario analysis, design thinking and augmented intelligence, and so on. Augmented intelligence is an alternative conceptualisation of artificial intelligence (AI). While AI plays an assistive role in advancing human capabilities, "augmented intelligence reflects the ongoing impact of artificial intelligence in amplifying human innovation" (Araya, 2019). There is a conundrum for both sources (machine and human) of SCSP, however. It is that inevitably both will be influenced by varying degrees of bias.

The incidence of bias in human strategic thinking

Of critical importance to strategy practice is an understanding of cognitive biases that arise from changes in the philosophical dimensions of space and time. This means that the validity of intuition, instinct and 'gut feel' must be called into question, especially when considered in the futuristic context of strategy. As less informed dimensions of strategy practice, history has shown that these decidedly unstructured sources of decision making have long been acceptable, even if dubious in nature.

Golden's (1992) research findings of relevance to bias found, for example, that a surprisingly strong degree of bias exists in human cognitive consciousness, especially with retrospection where memories of the past act as a basis to project potential outcomes into the future. Golden's observations show that in any application, not just strategy, retrospection is problematic. The concern, Golden (1992) suggested, lies in the fact that memories of the past, which by definition are an interpretation of the 'supposed' reality of yesterday and today, are an unreliable foundation upon which humans can evolve/conceptualise reliable fortuitive 'memories of the future'.

Retrospection, Golden (1992) suggested, is a term that is used to describe our ability to re-experience the past. In contrast, the opposite of retrospection, prospection is a term he used to 'pre-experience' the future. Interestingly, all animals, Golden observed, can predict pleasurable or unpleasant (hedonic) consequences of experience. Only humans, however, can predict hedonic events not previously experienced. This is accomplished via programs of simulations in our minds. He concluded that

> *humans are good at remembering the good times and the bad times, but not the run of the mill times – and therein lies one problem of bias.*

How often have you fallen victim to the statements "this is the way the last CEO did it, and it worked well, but she has gone now", and "we tried that before; it nearly blew up the factory".

Gilbert and Wilson (2007) provided further insight. They observed quite literally that humans often rely on retrospection (memories of the past) to build new perceptions of the future. Such refections however may not be all that reliable. An example of this question of reliability Golden observed, is demonstrated by his research into recollections of strategy content recalled by CEOs. In his findings, he noted

> *of those CEOs who were asked to recount strategic postures adopted some two years prior, 58% did not agree they had adopted those strategies they had actually followed at that time.*

Clearly, strategy practitioners need to be conscious of how past recollections (hindsight) are applied to make decisions about the future (foresight) based on an interpretation of 'what is' today (insight).

Many other forms of bias exist and have been identified by Lovallo and Sibony (2010). Some examples include the following:

• **Action-oriented biases:** The incidence of excessive optimism, overconfidence

- **Interest biases:** Incidence of conflicting incentives, nonmonetary and emotional
- **Stability biases:** Create a tendency towards inertia in the presence of uncertainty
- **Status quo biases:** Preference for the status quo in the absence of pressure to change it

The incidence of bias in machine learning and artificial intelligence

For all its promised benefits, there is an emerging reality that machine learning and artificial intelligence has a problem with bias: "AI can help reduce bias, but it can also bake in and scale bias", according to McKinsey artificial intelligence specialists Silberg and Manyika (2019). Their views have been confirmed on many occasions as practitioners as august as Stephen Hawking (Rutschman, 2018), for example, have warned against such issues as racial or gender bias in various applications. Instances where bias in artificial intelligence will have an impact include job interviews, mortgage applications, candidature for surveillance by law enforcement and security services or eligibility for parole. Similarly, data entered into an AI-driven analytical tool can be subject to built-in bias despite best efforts of the artificial intelligence programmers. As an example, it has been found that bias created within an artificial intelligence system can later become amplified as the algorithms evolve. It will be necessary, therefore, to develop the means to minimise the probability that bias will be introduced into artificial intelligence algorithms, either through externally supplied data or from within.

In general, artificial intelligence enables machines to learn more over time. Initially, an algorithm might make decisions using only a relatively simple set of calculations based on a small number of data sources. As the artificial intelligence system learns from experience, it can also broaden the amount and variety of data it uses as input and subjects that data to increasingly sophisticated processing. This means that an algorithm will likely end up being much more complex than when it was initially deployed. Notably, these changes are not due to human intervention designed to modify the code but rather to automatic modifications made by the machine based on its own behaviour. When commenting on bias in artificial intelligence capabilities, IBM (2019) observed on its website,

> Bias in AI system mainly occurs in the data or in the algorithmic model that underpins it. As AI systems we can trust are developed further, it's critical to develop and train these systems with data that is unbiased and to develop algorithms that can be easily explained.

Application of deep critical thinking

Critical thinking is a mode of cognition that can be applied to any subject, content or problem in which the thinker improves the quality of his or her thinking. They do this by skilfully analysing, assessing and reconstructing the core content of the topic under review. Critical thinking is, according to The Foundation for Critical Thinking (2019), enacted in a form that is "self-directed, self-disciplined, self-monitored, and self-corrective". Its practice presupposes assent to rigorous standards of excellence and a mindful command of their use. It also entails effective communication and problem-solving abilities, as well as a commitment to overcome our natural tendency towards native egocentrism and sociocentrism and bias.

Conduct of open strategy practice

Traditionally in government and business, strategy has been the sole domain of the respective corporate and business unit leadership, professional corporate strategy practitioners and management consultants. Increasingly, this is no longer the case. As suggested in Chapter 1, one of the strongest emergent trends in Strategy Evaluation in general has been the introduction of the concept of open strategy practice.

Whittington et al. (2011) point to four forces that contribute to the increasing use of open strategy in organisations.
They are:

Organisation: a crumbling of organisational boundaries and herarchies
Societal shifts: towards managerial egalitarianism and mobility
Culture: popularisation of strategy, and
Technology: new technologies that set information free

In his presentation at an international conference held in London in late 2017, Whittington challenged delegates to nominate "who would be the leader in the uptake of open strategy practice". Would it be consultants, business strategy practitioners or academics? Offering coincidental insight to the answer, Paul Foley, past CSO at Vodafone Ireland, was already there. In his presentation, he suggested that the best way to capture this set of independent activities within an organisation is through

> *the conduct of a consultative, collaborative and iterative approach to strategy practice.*

In another presentation at the same conference, this one held in Melbourne, Senior Executive Anthony Claridge advised the audience to 'openly' share their approach and content when developing strategy content. Claridge suggested that practitioners frame issues in a way that can be useful for employees to think in a broader way:

> *"Always give them the opportunity to think left and/or right about an issue", he suggested.*

We will discuss the practical application of open strategy as a practice in more detail in Chapter 6.

Strategy Evaluation, Reviewing: assessing the value and effectiveness of strategy

The content of Strategy Evaluation, Reviewing is demonstrated on the right hand side of Figure 3.3. As stated previously, an evaluation of strategy effectiveness must focus as much on the assumptions and estimates that went into decision making as it does on an assessment of the value or benefit of outcomes and results. Content that is included in a Strategy Evaluation, Reviewing capability is determined by the extent to which a loss of relevance, or similar outcome, will impact the strategy practitioners ongoing confidence in some, or all of the strategy's validity or value. Early investors in Blockchain-enabled cryptocurrencies, such as Bitcoin and Ethereum, for example, made some big assumptions about its future success. They include the acceptance of its validity as a legal currency, uptake by potential customers and that the technology would work. No doubt, those who did make the plunge were watching these three factors pretty closely as its fortunes have waxed and waned since its launch.

The implementation of a Strategy Evaluation, Reviewing monitoring capability will be undertaken as an essential and critical component of the Program of Continual Strategy Renewal. This construct and the treatment of its components are explored and explained further in Chapter 4. The specific program where this activity takes place is the Strategy Monitoring and Renewal Mechanism (Figure 4.5).

Strategy Evaluation, Reviewing: establishing a corporate university

Another and separate objective of a Strategy Evaluation, Reviewing is the capture and dissemination of knowledge obtained from the lessons learned from ongoing strategising activities. In the establishment of a strategy and transformation group at SPPD, Jenny and Alicia agreed that they would invite Charles Bakersfield to assume responsibility for the coordination and delivery of all learning and development activities, as well as aged-care strategy formulation and implementation. He would similarly be responsible for ensuring that SPPD strategy was well understood and incorporated into everything they did.

As a learning and development function in particular, he was also asked to ensure that lessons learned from the formal Strategy Evaluation, Shaping and Reviewing activities would be incorporated and embedded in the Organisational Learning Knowledge Database. In this format, Jenny and Alicia reasoned, Charles's function could eventually end up as a corporate university. It was a little early to float that idea at this stage though. Even so, the learning and development function along with strategy and transformation would still be required to lead and coordinate all learning and development activities, projects undertaken, knowledge accumulated and learning disseminated.

Evolving a Strategy Narrative and redefined journey of transformation at SPPD

The fundamentals of the Strategy Narrative, Strategy Blueprint and proposed approach to implementation were well informed by the backcasting exercise referred to previously. It was based on the observation from Chapter 2 that an ambidextrous program of strategic transformation would enable both the strengthening of its core business and the evolution of the foundations for SPPD to transform to a new business at the same time. It was the ideal solution for Jenny, Alicia thought. It would allow SPPD to strengthen its core business while at the same time contribute to its transformation to a new high-tech, customer-focused, agile division of T-wI.

The opportunity existed now, therefore, for the executive team to immediately expand the dynamics of the two streams of transformation described in Chapter 2. The chosen program would be the starting point of its revised strategy journey. A more expansive explanation of each pathway was developed and incorporated into Alicia's continued development of a formal Strategy Narrative as follows:

Pathway 1: Agile Adaptation: Nurture and optimise core business:

- **Posture: passive evolution:** Evaluate options as an adapter to change. Initial correction to cost structure and organisation structure. Promotion of cautious growth subject to cash constraints and executive capabilities
- **Action: adoption of low-risk options:** Decisions that yield significant positive pay-offs. Initial cautious growth steadily building to a state of rapid transformation in alignment with Pathway 2
  Primary objectives from establishing this first pathway they resolved would be to

  - improve the efficiency and effectiveness of core business by restructuring, cutting costs and rationalising the product range;
  - invest in technology aimed at the introduction of automation and elimination of unnecessary costs in manufacturing processes, as well as back-office support;
  - satisfy consumer expectations that SPPD is reducing its reliance on plastics; and
  - satisfy growth requirements through investment in innovation and a search for complementary 'bolt-on' acquisitions designed to grow market share in existing business areas

  Objectives and expected outcomes would include

  - a reduction in costs, improved customer satisfaction and short term operating performance while at the same time funding the roll-out of the second stream of the pathway to the future;

- a critical assessment of all opportunities available from new technology;
- an appreciation of all issues associated with the introduction of plastic substitutes;
- immediate development of an environmental nurturing program allowing SPPD to buy enough time to:
  - build its image as a socially responsible and environmentally friendly company,
  - identify solutions that will provide SPPD with substitute products; and
  - introduce a monitoring system allowing it to assess critical 'trigger' points of change

Pathway 2: Deliberate Disruption: Transform to emerging business:

- **Posture: (cautious) shape the future:** Exploration of evolutionary but rapid transformation through the adoption of Third Wave Strategy practice
- **Action: Deliberate Disruption**: Focused strategies with positive, sometimes negative pay-offs. Exploration of, and initially cautious investment in, multidextrous opportunity research and realisation of rapid organisational transformation drawing on the
  - conduct of deeper research into the implications of the timing and profitability of 'smart packaging' and other related technology,
  - identify opportunities to capitalise on existing capabilities – realise quick wins, and
  - identify competences required to support SPPD's move to introduce 'big bet' ventures using broad-based and advanced technology when the time is right (monitored through appropriate trigger points)

Primary objectives from establishing Pathway 1, they resolved, would be to allow SPPD to take advantage of both re and prosponsive opportunities as they arise. Accordingly, a revised Strategy Narrative describing their Short Term Strategy was built around a Strategic Change Agenda of "transform to a high performance, sponsive personalised service provider". In their preparation of the Strategy Narrative, a further revision of the divisional structure was deemed appropriate. The question was, should the organisation structure follow the recognition of the three market domains of health, consumer goods and finance? The answer was yes. It would be necessary if it hoped to obtain a greater concentration on market representation. As demonstrated in Figure 3.5, a Strategy Blueprint was developed to reflect content contained in the Strategy Narrative.

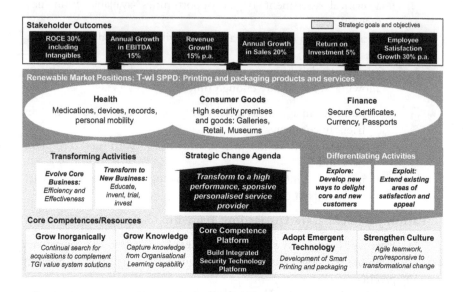

Figure 3.5 Short term SPPD strategy presented in the form of a Strategy Blueprint

Enhancing SPPD strategy – a revised program, a revised Strategic Architecture

Adoption of Pathway 2 was a different story. Encouraged by the new ideas and strategic insights that had become apparent since their early discussions, Jenny could now see that the transformation of SPPD into a value-oriented Hyper – HPO was not only plausible but possible. The recent ambidextrous approach articulated by the team she considered carried a strong capacity for uniqueness and inclusiveness, which she could pursue through the development of a customer-focused Integrated Value System.

Jenny joined the leadership team in their embracing of the idea of incorporating high technology into their operations as well. In particular, she saw the opportunity to introduce a far greater personalisation and systemisation of their services. She moved immediately to formalise the establishment of the three divisions of health, consumer goods and finance while at the same time seeking to introduce at least the sentiment of a Dynamic Market System. She immediately changed the name of the division from T-wI, SPPD to T-wI, Personalised Security Division (PSD). Staying with the Strategic Intent of "integrated provider of personalised security systems", the Strategic Architecture illustrated in Figure 2.11 was retained as a representation of Long Term Strategy for PSD.

Jenny's next move was to immediately appoint Alicia to the leadership role of the newly formed PSD in the role of Executive Director, T-wI, PSD – Health. Alicia wasted no time in developing a Long Term Strategy and Strategic Architecture with her team. It appears as Figure 3.6.

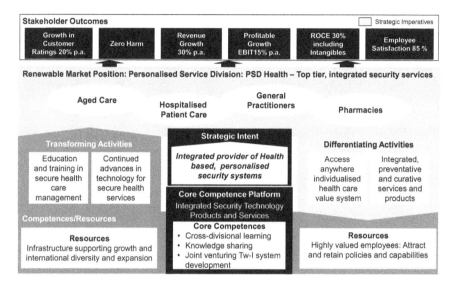

Figure 3.6 Strategic Architecture, PSD – Health

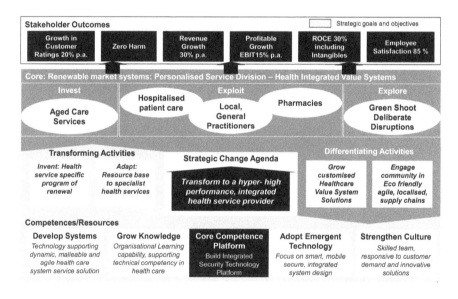

Figure 3.7 Strategy Blueprint for emergent business of T-wI, PSD – Health

The ensuing Strategic Architecture was quickly followed with the formalisation of its short term Strategy Narrative and its extrapolation into a Strategy Blueprint (illustrated in Figure 3.7). In its design, Alicia and her divisional team sought to pursue a Strategic Change Agenda that focused on the establishment of the service provision in the form of a quasi-Dynamic Market System. It focused on addressing four key areas of PSD – Health; they were aged care, hospitalised patient care, general practitioners and pharmacies. Confident that the Long Term Strategy for the division was now confirmed and agreed at the highest levels, Alicia's primary task was to implement the Short Term Strategy. This, she considered was tantamount to the introduction of an organisational transformation program. The Strategic Change Agenda that now lay at the heart of the Short Term Strategy was concise: "Transform to a hyper – high performance, integrated health service provider".

4   Implementing Third Wave Strategy

Chapter overview

We propose and present in this chapter a meaningful method of implementing strategy – one that is based on an assumption of continual renewal as opposed to a static, ritualised, annual strategic plan. Our alternative is presented and discussed in this chapter within the context of a dynamic Program of Continual Strategy Renewal. Conducted within the context of a Pathway to Transformation and 'agile' work practices, there are three elements of the program of renewal. They are Stakeholder Engagement, Strategy Monitoring and Renewal and a Strategic Change Program.

The first is Stakeholder Engagement; it is the change management program applied to ensure that strategy is accepted and owned by all stakeholders. The second is Strategy Monitoring and Renewal; it is there to ensure that strategy remains relevant and that lessons of commission, omission and irrelevance are learned and captured. This is the program where Strategy Evaluation, Reviewing, is of greatest concern. The third is the role of the Strategic Change Program. It is included to ensure that Short Term Strategy is implemented in a professional manner. The ongoing monitoring and reporting of each of these activities, as well as the Strategy Narrative and Strategy Blueprint, is captured within a formal and embedded dashboard-designed reporting mechanism that is referred to as a performance measurement, management, monitoring and reporting mechanism.

Learning insights

The successful implementation of strategy has long eluded strategy practitioners who on the whole have been more responsible for its formulation rather than implementation. An often heard cry, however, is that "all the strategy in the world is useless if it isn't implemented properly". As you will have observed in this book so far, however, implementation is much more than a 'to-do' list or mega program management capability. It is for this reason that the people issue of Stakeholder Engagement is included here as a critical component of strategy implementation. It is also a good reason to include a monitoring and renewal program, without which we may never know if its relevance is maintained and our gut feeling left itching. Finally, it is also a reason to include a formal program and project management capability; one that is designed to ensure that strategic projects are treated like any other projects and managed accordingly.

From a technical perspective, each of the elements of the Program of Continual Strategy Renewal and associated mechanisms are described in this Chapter. Associated mechanisms include a context of organisational transformation in the form of a Pathway to Transformation. They also include a description and illustration of a stepped approach to the introduction of agile work practices. From a practical perspective, we again demonstrate the application of conceptual ideas to practice through our review of the new PSD – Health division of T-wI.

Once again, this case study demonstrates the iterative nature of strategy and the many disruptions to a journey of transformation and renewal that may occur as new knowledge comes to light and early decisions are made to look less valuable than they were first thought to be. Fundamental to the guidance given to the PSD – Health leadership team are the strategy tools that have been presented to ground original thought and provide a structure to a depth of strategic thinking.

Work plan phase 4: implementing Third Wave Strategy

As demonstrated in Table 0.1 the exploratory work plan for strategy formulation now follows the methodology contained in the Third Wave Strategy framework. It involves a hands-on approach to Strategy Implementation. The work plan of relevance to our proposed method of Strategy Implementation is encapsulated within a Program of Continual Strategy Renewal (Figure 4.1).

Introduction: implementing a Program of Continual Strategy Renewal at PSD – Health

Alicia Manning, newly appointed executive director for T-wI, PSD – Health, had by now become quite comfortable with the idea of taking responsibility for a transformation project that would spearhead positive change across the division and then the corporation. Her real test, however, was starting to emerge. Presenting the PSD – Health Strategy Narrative and Strategy Blueprint to the T-wI board of directors was daunting enough. Now she needed to garner the support of all stakeholders as the mode of strategy practice rolled over from an emphasis on formulation to that of implementation and continual renewal.

Emboldened by the fact that her task was nowhere near as pressing as those that many other senior leaders in the corporate world faced, she likened her

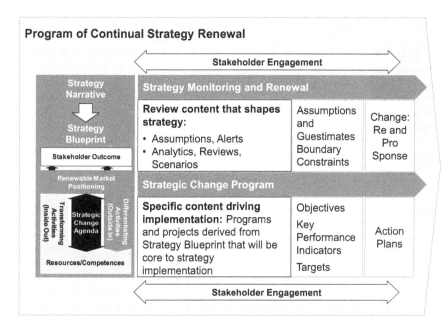

Figure 4.1 Phase 4: development and delivery of a strategy and leadership development program at SPPD: a Program of Continual Strategy Renewal

challenge to that of the CEO of the Ford Motor Company, Jim Hackett. His organisational transformation plan (Ford, 2018) was bolstered by the existence of a reliable and solid core business which would generate a sustainable cash flow for some time. It wasn't all plain sailing for Hackett, however.

> *Ford didn't have the luxury of putting its toe in the water with a pilot program; it was all or nothing for him and the board of directors, and they knew it.*

Shrugging off a fear of failure

Despite all the assurances from supporters, Alicia was a little shaken by the news that not too far into the transformation program that had commenced in 2018, Ford announced its annual results. They were 50% lower than the previous year. Amidst an estimated $11 billion restructuring charge, Hackett repeatedly sought to reassure analysts that all was well. Suggesting that 2018 should be seen as "the year between the business that wasn't designed right and the business that we know will win" (Waldmeir, 2019), Hackett gave little away as to the overall progress of the restructuring project that he had instigated.

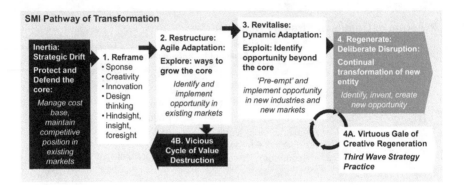

Figure 4.2 Emerging out of a state of inertia: a Pathway of Transformation at PSD – Health

Instead of panicking, Alicia was able to demonstrate her strength as a leader. She shrugged off the doubts and pressed on with the development of the restructuring component of PSD – Health's Pathway of Transformation, first presented in the companion book (*Corporate Strategy (Remastered) I*) and demonstrated here in Figure 4.2.

Alicia was satisfied that the enormous amount of time that she had spent in the first activity of reframing had been worthwhile. Her immediate thoughts, however, were focused on ensuring that she could find a balance between the need to restructure the core business while at the same time investing wisely in the area that had recently been confirmed as subject of the pilot project; that of aged care. Accordingly, she noted, she would need to keep a close watch on the design of the ensuing revitalisation program once the restructuring process had been completed. Based on an expectation that the pilot program in aged care would be successful, it was vital that the expansion of that program in the revitalisation stage of the Pathway of Transformation (Figure 4.2) could be used to complete the transformation of the entire division into the final episode of regeneration and, ideally, hyper – high performance. Although Alicia hadn't changed PSD – Health's statements of purpose and mission, the ambition she shared with her team was encapsulated in a new vision statement:

PSD – Health Vision: To be recognised as world leaders in delivery of health-related, high-value assets and document security systems.

Alicia wasn't proposing a one-off change though. What she had volunteered for was the pioneering of a program of organisational transformation and renewal that would eventually be implemented across the entire company.

The ultimate objective for the corporate business was the realisation of continual regeneration and the emergence of the business as a Hyper – HPO.

Launching the Strategy Implementation/organisational transformation program

Treating the foregoing outcome as a priority, Alicia and recently appointed Executive General Manager, Strategy and Transformation, Charles Bakersfield, elected to commence the exercise with a program to be extracted from what they thought would be a final Strategy Blueprint for the aged care business. Illustrated in Figure 4.3, the members of the leadership team were comfortable with the fact that they were now ready to include the notion of a Dynamic Market System as a part of an Integrated Value System into their thinking. The Strategic Change Agenda to be included in this revised Strategy Blueprint was "transform to a hyper – high performance, integrated aged care services provider".

Implementing a Program of Continual Strategy Renewal at PSD – Health aged care

Alicia was also more comfortable now that she knew what the design of the restructuring component of the overall strategy transformation and renewal system would look like. She informed Charles that she would leave it to him to manage that activity. In accepting the offer, Charles would be guided mostly by the construct that follows the Strategy Blueprint (Figure 4.3) and Program of Continual Strategy Renewal (Figure 4.1). One of the key challenges he faced, however, was a lack of detail regarding the specifics of each project to be undertaken.

Although he had been warmly welcomed to PSD – Health because of his understanding of emergent digital technologies, he was concerned that there was much to explore and understand about them and their application to PSD – Health and aged care specifically. Before they could be definitively applied to the PSD – Health technology portfolio, they would need to be thoroughly tested and reviewed. Charles went to great lengths, therefore, to impress upon anyone who would listen, especially Jenny and Alicia, that the projects to be conducted would be more exploratory than conclusive.

They would also, he stressed, be of relevance to both pathways to implementation. Blockchain, for example, promised to enhance the Pathway 1 core business improvement program by reducing international financial transaction costs by some 40%. At the same time, it would reduce transaction processing time by 80%. Its greatest value, however, could be derived from the Pathway 2 transformation program, which Charles estimated could provide the foundation for a division-wide Core Competence Platform. This technology, he suggested, could ultimately provide the underlying technology for the entire T-wI security-focused Integrated Value System. Blockchain would, he assured them, provide a new level of security and authentication to PSD – Health in the areas of documentation, authentication and legitimisation. It could also be leveraged into high-value branded goods, jewellery and financial instruments, as well as secure documents. This was in fact *the* key feature of a Blockchain technology overall.

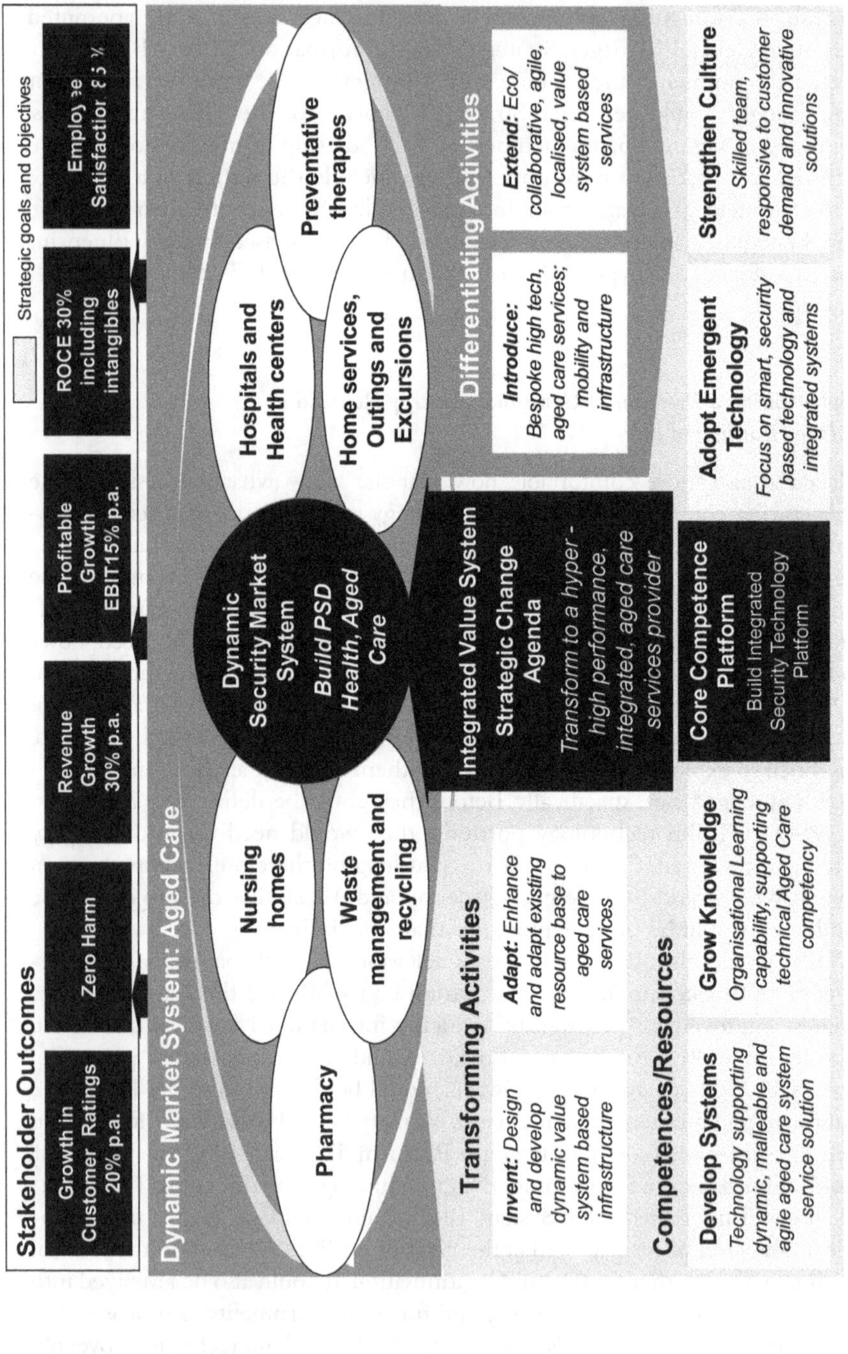

Stakeholder Outcomes

Strategic goals and objectives

| Growth in Customer Ratings 20% p.a. | Zero Harm | Revenue Growth 30% p.a. | Profitable Growth EBIT15% p.a. | ROCE 30% including intangibles | Employee Satisfaction 85% |

Dynamic Market System: Aged Care

Dynamic Security Market System
Build PSD Health, Aged Care

- Preventative therapies
- Hospitals and Health centers
- Home services, Outings and Excursions
- Nursing homes
- Waste management and recycling
- Pharmacy

Integrated Value System
Strategic Change Agenda
Transform to a hyper-high performance, integrated, aged care services provider

Transforming Activities

Invent: Design and develop dynamic value system based infrastructure

Adapt: Enhance and adapt existing resource base to aged care services

Differentiating Activities

Introduce: Bespoke high tech, aged care services; mobility and infrastructure

Extend: Eco/ collaborative, agile, localised, value system based services

Competences/Resources

Develop Systems
Technology supporting dynamic, malleable and agile aged care system service solution

Grow Knowledge
Organisational Learning capability, supporting technical Aged Care competency

Core Competence Platform
Build Integrated Security Technology Platform

Adopt Emergent Technology
Focus on smart, security based technology and integrated systems

Strengthen Culture
Skilled team, responsive to customer demand and innovative solutions

Figure 4.3 A detailed depiction of the Strategy Blueprint for T-wI, PSD – Health, aged care

Jenny and Alicia were both heartened by this update from Charles. They resolved, therefore, to take a cautious approach to the design of the reinvented aged care division. Rather than risking everything on untried and untested technology, however, they elected to progress with a vision for aged care that was based on a conceptual Integrated Value System as described in their newly revised Strategy Blueprint shown in Figure 4.3.

A much relieved Charles was now motivated to move forward with the implementation of the proposed Program of Continual Strategy Renewal. It would not be in ignorance of emerging technology, however. Rather, it would be conducted with the knowledge that emerging technology was evolving and that PSD – Health was very much committed to the uptake of that technology but only when it was appropriate and viable financially. The PSD – Health leadership teams objective now, therefore, was to get through the restructuring and revitalisation stages of the Pathway of Transformation (Figure 4.2) and to move on to regeneration. Charles was now ready to launch the implementation program. It would commence with the design and operation of an agile approach to Stakeholder Engagement.

Conducting a Stakeholder Engagement program at aged care

Alicia felt that the one task that she couldn't ask Charles to do was to take control of the Stakeholder Engagement program on his own. That would, she felt, be a critical component of the success of the entire transformation initiative and would require the visibility of, and commitment from, the entire leadership team and her participation in person. Leading the charge, the first challenge she identified as critical to the success of the program was the overhaul of the aged care's organisational culture. This was also an issue of concern to Jenny Wong; it was an issue which she had already recognised as a key priority for the entire division. Jenny, Alicia and Charles resolved to handle this as a joint exercise to be run out of the division office with the support of the corporate office. Above all else, each were conscious of the fact that the strategy should inform and direct the substance of the culture change program as well.

Introducing agile into Strategy Implementation

As with the purpose of transformation, Charles and Alicia sought to incorporate the idea of an 'agile' approach to the Strategy Implementation activities and, accordingly, the Stakeholder Engagement component of the journey. We propose agile as a vehicle for Stakeholder Engagement because it is a specialist and learned skill which provides it with credibility and longevity. Because of its embrace of openness and engagement, it is also highly influential in bringing about a culture change and the introduction of an open strategy practice, when appropriate. As an organisation-wide, all-encompassing philosophy, it naturally incorporates a broad range of stakeholders in its operation. It is, therefore, a tool that will more than satisfy inclusion, promote a positive and vibrant culture and provide a method of engagement that will ensure buy-in and ownership of outcomes and results (good and bad).

Consistent with their adoption of the philosophy of Strategy Evaluation, Reviewing, skills learned through the conduct of the aged care pilot project would be added to the organisational learning capability now being developed by Charles as a separate exercise. In describing the operation of an agile methodology, we adapt the description used by McKinsey and Company (2018) who described it as

> *a network of teams that operate in rapid learning and decision-making cycles.*

Each team, McKinsey suggested,

> *instils a common sense of purpose and use of new data.*

New purpose has already been accepted by Alicia and her team at PSD – Health. New data is being generated daily as the reframing and restructuring agenda has moved from brainstorming to practice. Both, however, will be applied to the PSD – Heath knowledge bank through the program of Strategy Evaluation, Reviewing and the Program of Continual Strategy Renewal, as explained in more detail later in this chapter. According to McKinsey, its value is released through "the empowerment of teams closest to the information with fast tracked decision rights". Ideally,

> *such teams will combine velocity and adaptability with stability and efficiency.*

In its adoption, Alicia recognised its success would be realised through the *empowerment of teams* delivered via the introduction of a pragmatic, agile and inclusive approach to its management. This combination, she thought, would be greatly assisted through the visible support, engagement, understanding and commitment by all stakeholders of each project.

To provide structure to this program, Alicia asked Charles to research what other organisations had done so that their team could learn from those experiences. One example that caught their attention was that of NASA. As mentioned in Chapter 1, NASA had found it possible to create fertile ground for the successful realisation of organisational change. It was achieved through the adoption of a series of structured and somewhat radical actions that are consistent and in full congruence with the philosophy of Third Wave Strategy and agile work practices. We have adapted the findings of authors (Heracleous et al., 2019) who observed the actions of a renegade group of change agents within NASA to our discussion here also.

As somewhat radical change agents, Heracleous et al. (2019) observed, this renegade group subsequently became known as 'the Pirates'. Examples of the essential fundamentals of the Pirates' approach to the implementation of 'unencumbered change' includes

- a culture not afraid of failure, encourages challenge and positive dissent;
- low or no resistance from bureaucracy, encourage experimentation;
- inspiration, motivation from the highest levels; and
- recognition for early wins to motivate others.

Arguably, agile methods of work are valuable when changes in the way businesses are structured and operated. It is highly appropriate to apply this to Strategy Implementation. It is also highly appropriate to consider strategising activities to be highly correlated with those associated with the conditions described by Repenning et al. (2018). These authors recognise that ambiguity plays an important role in work practices. Changes in work practices can, they suggested, can be recognised as being either

- non-ambiguous, operationally focused activities that are well defined and are the norm within 'business as usual' specific environments, or
- ambiguous, strategically focused activities that are non-routine and occur within ill-defined organisational situations and environments.

Taking Toyota as an example, Repenning et al. (2018) suggested that non-ambiguous, operationally focused activities would typically be the tasks that include the workshop activities of adding parts on an assembly line or paint on a spray painting line. On occasion, however, these simple tasks can become ambiguous as the norm gives way to uncertainty. An example of this is a key feature of the Toyota manufacturing system. Referred to by Toyota (2006) on their UK/GB website as Andon, it is the situation when an operator in a workstation is empowered to halt the entire production line at his or her will. Such an act is encouraged following the occurrence of an unintended or unexpected event that would cause that operator or his or her workstation to fall behind.

   Unless this problem is addressed immediately, the entire production system can remain out of balance for some time. That situation would create a far greater problem than would the troubles being experienced by the single operator alone. The lines of control governing the production process in this instance the authors suggested, move from one of a well-defined level of predictability to one that is ill defined.

> *It is in the occurrence of this ambiguity that the authors propose that measures of agility are triggered and as a result induces those involved to move from a mode of individual, mechanistic control to that of collaborative modes of problem resolution.*

In managing such an incidence, the authors identified four principles that contribute to the creation of a shift in mechanisms – from static, well-defined tasks to ambiguous collaboratives. These points of differentiation are similar to those that prevail between static strategic planning and Third Wave Strategy practice. Repenning et al.'s approach is adapted, therefore, to the conduct of agile decision making in an ambiguous context of Strategy Implementation. An adaptation of a summary of the four steps identified by Repenning et al. and conducted within the context of Strategy Implementation are presented as follows:

1. **Identify and confirm areas of ambiguity.**
   Strategy Implementation consists of projects that are made up of newly defined work. By definition, decisions made to identify which tasks will be needed include those addressing what the Strategy Implementation projects will look like, how they will be conducted and the degree of ambiguity associated with them. This line of questioning will likely be accentuated in the early stages of the development of the Strategy Implementation projects and programs. That is because activities in the early stages will be ill defined and will, therefore, require further evaluation and clarification before a work program can be confirmed.

   In the initial stages of project definition, it is essential that the ensuing collaboration involves the engagement of all parties responsible for the implementation of strategy and in this case especially the ensuing transformation of the organisation. In our case, this will include designated members of the COSP.

2. **Break projects into smaller units of work that are more frequently checked.**
   Repenning et al. (2018) suggest that agility is dependent upon "the frequency and effectiveness with which output is assessed". In the context of Strategy Implementation, processes will be new and likely subject to uncertainty and ambiguity. In which case it will be useful to apply the fundamental rule of agility, which Repenning et al. suggested is to break projects down into smaller units of work. The reasoning behind this suggestion is that project monitoring (Strategy Evaluation, Reviewing) "is made easier because they can be checked more frequently".

3. **Identify the help chain of individuals who support those doing the work.**
   In addition to the assignment of responsibility, Repenning et al. suggested that the supervision of the projects will be made easier through the introduction of so-called help chains. The makeup of individuals in a help chain network are those who can actively support those doing the work. In strategy, members of the COSP, including the Systemic Cognitive Strategy Practitioners, could be assigned to a help chain for specific projects contributing to strategy formation, evaluation, implementation and alignment. In this case, it is not the roles, departments or functions of advisors that will be important to success Repenning et al. (2018) observed. Rather,

   it is the essence of the philosophy of agility that requires "knowing whom to call when there is a problem or feedback is needed".

4. **Introduce triggers and checks that move work into a collaborative mode.**

Once the help chain is established, the notion of Strategy Evaluation, Reviewing moves into project management mode, which in our case is the Strategy Monitoring and Renewal component of the Program of Continual Strategy Renewal. Its objective, consistent with agile operations, is to identify two basic mechanisms for activating evaluation. These mechanisms are referred to by Repenning et al. (2018) as triggers and checks.

"A trigger is a test that reveals defects or misalignment". In its application to strategy, we suggest that perceived problems requiring input and advice from the relevant collaborative strategy advisory team will be triggered by the appropriate project manager or relevant COSP practitioner(s). A key trigger, in the context of strategy, is when an assumption that was made to make a strategic decision turns out to be an incorrect one. If such an outcome is anticipated, then measures to address the situation will have been put in place. If the outcome is not expected, then measures of remediation will need to be stablished quickly. Awareness of an anticipated eventuality will become readily apparent if it is being monitored in the trend variation alerting mechanism, the structure of which is illustrated in Figure 4.6.

Here a check is established at prescheduled review points when the work is moved to a more collaborative environment for assessment. This happens, Repenning et al. (2018) suggested, "in daily meetings where the team quickly assesses the current state of the project". As will be seen later, the extent of checking is dependent upon the immediacy and importance of the strategic project being implemented.

Application of agile strategy practices to PSD – Health

In order to build momentum, Charles set about establishing project teams for each of the key strategic objectives identified in the Strategy Blueprint and described in detail in the Strategy Narrative. Fundamental to the success of the program was the construct of the Strategy Monitoring and Renewal mechanisms. Seeking a fresh approach to the design and management of these systems, Charles assigned responsibility for this task to the newly appointed Chief Technology Officer, Sanjay Barti. Along with this role, Sanjay was also invited to take responsibility for the implementation of the technology component of the PSD – Health transformation journey overall. Conscious of the need to establish a similar position in the change process in the core business, Charles asked Stephany Lee, newly appointed Group General Manager, Global Supply Chain, to also get involved.

All three leaders recognised that the objective was to get to a point of regeneration whereby the ambidextrous nature of the transformation would morph into a solid core whose objective was to seek multidextrous opportunities – and hyper – high performance. Their first priority, however, was to get through the current program of restructuring.

Implementing a Program of Continual Strategy Renewal

As illustrated in Figure 4.1 and as an extension of the Strategy Evaluation, Shaping and Reviewing regime (Chapter 3), practitioners will now be seeking to reassure themselves of two things. First is that the assumptions, estimates and guesstimates that went into the original Short Term Strategy development initiative remain relevant and legitimate. Second is that the projects identified as outcomes from the Strategy Narrative and articulated in the Strategy Blueprint are correctly managed and controlled. The construct of the mechanisms enabling this requirement is discussed next.

Strategy Monitoring and Renewal

The purpose of this mechanism is to ensure that strategy practitioners are prompted to continually review and, where appropriate, renew the fundamentals of the decisions that were made during the Strategy Evaluation, Shaping exercises (Chapter 3). These are the assumptions, estimates, guesstimates and, sometimes, forecasts that were also referred to previously.

As a strictly process-oriented, control mechanism, a specially designed spreadsheet mechanism can be developed to do the job; an example is presented as Figure 4.4. Its purpose is to ensure that leaders are made aware of the need to take either responsive or prosposive action in the most appropriate way, at the most appropriate time. As shown, the spreadsheet provides guidance to the Third Wave Strategy practitioner who will be interested to know what items of concern need to be reassessed, and when. Content to be included for scrutiny is typically based on decisions that were based on nothing more than intuition, hunches, hindsight, foresight and insight. Strategic decision making, however, needs more than intuition, a concept based on lessons learned from hindsight and insight. It also needs the input of foresight. In the absence of any word relating to future-oriented intuition, we have chosen to adopt the notion of fortuition. Fortuition will likely include content where less certain 'facts' and figures are deemed to be contentious and require ratification as the future unfolds. Whatever the source or cause of uncertainty, content included for review is listed in Column 1.

Some of the more obvious areas of uncertainty that are critical to success will no doubt already be under close scrutiny. Underlying strategic risk factors, however,

Program of Continual Strategy Renewal: Strategy Monitoring and Renewal						
Content of Strategy Narrative	Strategic Assumptions, Guesstimates and Estimates from Strategy Narrative	Priority	Expected Outcome	Current Trends/ Outcome	Action Item Ref.	Admin Officer
Adapt existing resource base to health services	• All resource base is suitable for adaptation	Orange	85% suitability	80% suitability	XYZ 001	Josh Steinbeck
	• Resource base is suitable for health services	Orange	60% suitability	55% suitability		
	• Adaptation will result in cost savings	Red	20% cost reduction	14% cost reduction		
	• No new technology is on horizon	Double red	New technology	Much better technology 2 years away		

Figure 4.4 Program of Continual Strategy Renewal: Strategy Monitoring and Renewal

should also be reviewed in order to provide advanced warning of changed circumstances. While some of the Short Term Strategy content will rely on the existence of a signed contract, for example, it is possible that a change in personnel, the arrival of advanced technology or the sudden emergence of competitors will lead to the contract not being honoured. It happens. This will quickly bring your best laid plans crashing to the ground. It will be useful, to assign priority rankings in order to highlight the greatest areas of risk as shown in Column 3 in the diagram. Although this simple representation does a good job, it could well be incorporated into an enterprise-wide performance management and reporting mechanism, as well as, or in addition to, some form of dashboard reporting capability.

Strategic Change Program

As noted previously, the Strategy Blueprint can only provide a high-level perspective of the content that will describe the sequence and details of the projects to be introduced as an outcome from the strategy content expressed in the Strategy Narrative. To get to the right level of detail, a second process-oriented worksheet can be developed. It could also be incorporated into an enterprise-wide reporting capability and dashboard reporting mechanism, if appropriate. Its objective, no matter which technology is deployed, is to organise and present details of the respective projects that are the outcome from the Strategy Narrative and then reflected in the Strategy Blueprint. Overall, it is a representation of the content that satisfies the objective of "implementing Long Term Strategy in the short term". An example is presented as Figure 4.5.

Each column presented in Figure 4.5 is described as follows:

Strategy Blueprint: strategic objectives: Guidance starts with an extrapolation of content contained in the Strategy Blueprint into the key component of the Program of Continual Strategy Renewal.

Assumptions made, ambiguity assessed: Assumptions may or may not be the same as those included in the performance measurement, management, monitoring and reporting system shown in Figure 4.7. At any rate, they are the assumptions that led to the acceptance of a specific strategic objective to be approved for implementation as part of the overall Strategy Implementation program. At the point of assessment, it is useful to assess the extent of ambiguity that will be associated with each project and thereby the appropriate action to be taken.

Projects from the Strategy Blueprint: These are the specific projects to be conducted that have been identified as actions required to ensure that the strategic objectives are implemented.

Current trends/outcomes and checkpoints: These two columns provide insight into any variations that may be expected to occur between the planned outcomes and the potential of those expectations to change. Should the variation become significant and require a higher profile of monitoring, they should be included in a live dashboard-based trend variation alerting mechanism consistent with that illustrated as Figure 4.6. In

	T-wl Personal Security Division (PSD) - Health				
	Program of Continual Strategy Renewal: Agile Strategic Change Program				
Strategy Blueprint: Strategic objectives	Assumptions and assessment of ambiguity	Projects from Strategy Blueprint	Current Trends/ Outcomes	Expected Outcome and Check Points	Responsible Officer and Help Chain member
1. Transforming activities: **Adapt existing resource base to health services** 70% of Health Division is already operating in the health industry. Our task will be to develop a new business framework and organisational design.	Benefits of efficiency, effectiveness will result in improved quality, lower cost base and each of the items outlined in the Strategy Narrative and business case that led to the decision to embrace the transformation. **Ambiguity: High**	2.1 Design and develop health industry value system for: • Aged care • Hospitalised patient care • General practitioners • Pharmacies	Significant trend towards introduction of Third Wave strategy practice, Agile Organisation structuring and uptake of advanced technology, in particular digitised technological solutions.	All benefits identified in Strategy Narrative: Agility, cost reductions, quality, speed of service delivery, faster product development. **Check point:** to be established at each point of project sign off.	**Leader:** Peter Appleyard **Help Chain:** Joe McDonald Mary Wi Christine Ling Henry Brown Jerry Steinberg
2. Transforming activities: Improve efficiency and effectiveness of core business We expect to close around 15% of manufacturing sites around the world and as result reduce overheads including head count.	New technology deemed appropriate will be available and working when required. **Ambiguity: High** Investments in will meet TgI Return on Investment criteria of 15% for each piece of technology **Ambiguity: Low**	1 Develop plan to introduce production optimisation program 2 Evaluate opportunities: supply chain optimisation 3 Rationalise product portfolio	2% Site Closures m and head count reduction by end of this year Supply Chain cost increasing by 2%	15% Site closures by 2022 20% lower head count by 2020 Supply Chain cost reduced by 10% **Check point:** to be established at each point of project sign off.	**Leader:** Mohamad Abdula **Help Chain:** Joe McDonald Mary Wi Melissa Orcado Joe Cincinnato Andrew Brown Beth Stein

Figure 4.5 Program of Continual Strategy Renewal: Strategic Change Program

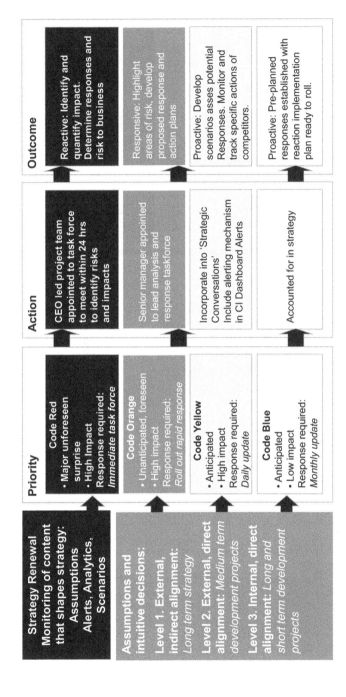

Figure 4.6 Program of Continual Strategy Renewal, trend variation alerting mechanism

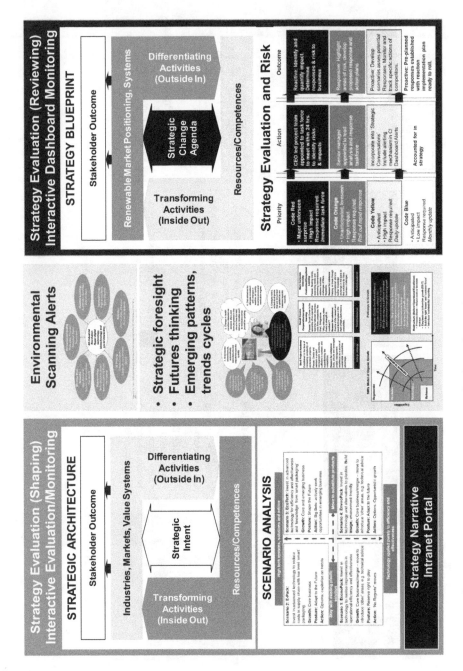

Figure 4.7 Performance measurement, management, monitoring and reporting system

an assessment of when and where an assessment needs to be clarified, an appropriate checkpoint should be established to flag the need for review.

Responsible officer and help chain member: Literally, the identification and contact details for agile team members responsible for supporting those doing the tasks identified as part of the Program of Continual Strategy Renewal.

Strategy performance measurement, management and reporting mechanism

As an enabler of Strategy Evaluation, Reviewing this final component of the Program of Continual Strategy Renewal represents the physical means by which the monitoring and renewal of strategy is conducted. An illustration of a formal performance measurement, management, monitoring and reporting system is presented in Figure 4.7.

Although purely illustrative, it is expected that this mechanism will, above all else, considerably enhance the control function of the managers and leaders responsible for the performance of strategy and business. Based on a management accountant's perception of a typical reporting function, the fully automated dashboard monitoring mechanism can also be developed in highly advanced technology or in basic spreadsheets. Either way, what it is intended to do is to demonstrate the essential pieces of information that will be demanded by those responsible for the strategic management of the business.

In demonstrating the essential components of Third Wave Strategy monitoring in this chapter, practitioners should be aware that there will be many variations in content selected for inclusion in or exclusion from this mechanism. It will also be tailored to the needs of each specific entity.

To clarify, illustrative content is included in each column presented in the construct illustrated in Figure 4.7:

Column 1: Long Term Strategy: Strategic Architecture and summary scenario analysis

Column 2: a mix of topics of contemporary strategic importance: These include highlighted topics of relevance, such as environmental scanning analysis, other charts and reports that provide information concerning various items of importance

Column 3: Short Term Strategy: Content that includes the Strategy Blueprint and alerting mechanism

Links to additional content are included as an email and social media–based communication mechanism. Underlying this structure is access to the Strategy Narrative and other sources of information of significance. Critical content will typically be pushed deliberately from internal sources. They may be internal business sourced from an ERP system or the company intranet. They could also come from external sources, also pushed towards this mechanism via a predetermined application sourced from a search engine, other online multi-media or from any other source of information in an electronic format – or not.

5   Strategic Alignment

Chapter overview

As a somewhat ill-defined topic, we introduce you initially to the concept of Alignment as a mechanism that brings together consequential and conflicting points of view. They arise in various attributes of strategy, such as objectives, tactics and, indeed, strategies themselves. To this extent, a number of "potential external areas and 'sub-areas' of plausible touch points" are presented where alignment may or may not be found between either the firm and the external environment or within the firm. We also assess the issue of alignment within strategy practice itself, as there are often areas of conflict within these boundaries too. Examples include planned vs. emergent strategy and Inside Out vs. Outside In strategy.

Notable within PSD – Health is the need to maintain a strict alignment between the business and advanced technologies which provide opportunities to benefit from strategies of adaptation and invention. This causes the leadership team to once again reconsider, renew and recalibrate its approach to its program of organisational transformation and renewal. It also alerts them to the need to incorporate an alignment/misalignment alerting mechanism into their strategically focused performance measurement, management, monitoring and reporting mechanism.

Learning insights

The issue of Strategic Alignment is not well understood or explored in any meaningful way in the strategy literature. It is our experience, however, that when considered in the context of sponsive strategic change especially, it is potentially one of the most important aspects of Third Wave Strategy. This is exactly the conclusion that the leadership team at PSD – Health reached as they grappled with both the threats and opportunities that advances in technology are bringing to their world. There are no specific approaches to an assessment of alignment upon which a universal methodology can be applied. In our exploration of Alignment in this chapter, therefore, we provide insight into, and examples of, areas of alignment and misalignment that could occur at any one of the three levels of engagement discussed in past chapters. By way of a reminder, Level 1 is an Outside In external indirect alignment, Level 2 is an Outside In external direct alignment and Level 3 is an Inside Out internal alignment. At Level 1 and 2, the greatest area of concern is the long standing and classic strategic issue of alignment between corporate strategy and influences exerted by the external environment. At Level 3, on the other hand, the greatest area of concern is an assessment of alignment between strategy and operations. As a broad-based issue, therefore, an exploration of examples of boundaries around which various touch points may present areas of weakness – or not was deemed appropriate. All of which could demand that strategy practitioners take appropriate measures to manage and control intended and unintended consequences that may arise from issues of alignment.

As specialist strategy practitioners, we also identify a number of areas where a lack of alignment in strategy theory could give rise to serious consequences. We identify and present four specific areas of strategy where evidence of such misalignment may be found. They are those of corporate structuring, network partnering, international strategy and organising. It should be noted that other areas can be found or become apparent from time to time.

Work plan phase 5: Strategic Alignment

We refer again to Figure 0.1 and our further explanation (Figure 0.3) that we use to describe our chapter structure and construct of Third Wave Strategy. In this chapter, we now address the issue of Strategic Alignment, as demonstrated in Figure 5.1. Here we review this issue from an Outside In and Inside Out perspective.

Introduction: addressing issues of Strategic Alignment

In addressing issues of Alignment, we differentiate between the early stages of an emerging corporation's trajectory and that of a mature corporation. For emerging corporations, the issue of Strategic Alignment is quite simple. Errors in assumptions aside, it either succeeds in its strategic goals and objectives or it doesn't. In other words, the outcomes are directly aligned with strategy or they're not. Similarly, as relatively small entities at the time of their establishment, there is usually little room for one part of the organisation and another to engage in conflicting activities. Amazon is a case in point, as demonstrated in Case example 5.1.

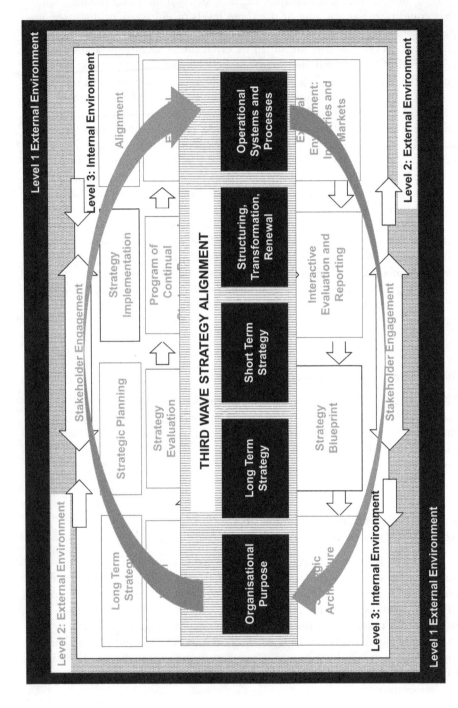

Figure 5.1 Phase 5: alignment between purpose, strategy, structure and operations in context of the Third Wave Strategy framework

---

Case example 5.1: Customer obsession as the driver of Strategic Alignment at Amazon

At the beginning of Amazon's journey, CEO Jeff Bezos defined a purpose for his business. it was: 'the everything store'. His vision was to establish an online retailer that was readily accessible and low in cost. Although he started with books, his intention was to ultimately sell a broad range of consumer items over the Internet. True to his vision, Bezos set about building an online bookshop, which he saw as a viable foundation for a new company using new technology to disrupt a very traditional industry. As an early mover into online trading, many were sceptical about such an idea. Members of the business press especially were harsh judges. One commentator in particular was keen to report his prediction of the demise of the Amazon venture. Judging it to be on the brink of bankruptcy, the journalist had assumed that the soon-to-be online presence of the 30,000-employee and $3-billion book retailer Barnes & Noble would swamp the 125-employee and $60-million (sales) Amazon (Kirby and Stewart, 2007).

In dealing with the apparent lack of faith, Bezos advised Amazon employees not to be overly worried. Rather, he suggested, they should be more concerned about Amazon's customers than competitors. That is because, Bezos stressed "they are the folks who have the money. Our competitors are never going to send us money" Kirby and Stewart (2007). And so Amazon's alignment with its customers has remained the central core to its culture right through to today.

The strength of Bezos's obsession with the customer has ensured that everyone in the entire organisation is fervently attuned and responsive to the customer's every want and need. To this extent, it is highly consistent with the philosophy of Third Wave Strategy,

Amazon wins by aligning itself directly with its customers to form a continually growing and independent journey of company, market and industry creation, thereby making competition obsolete.

In the case of many mature and established organisations, the complexity of alignment seems to be unfathomable. As the years have passed size, structure and, indeed, organisational purpose will inevitably have become far more ambiguous and imprecise. As a result, the numerous and often disconnected stakeholders have succumbed to the conundrum of not being able to 'see the woods for the trees'. When considering those corporations facing these circumstances, it is apparent that the link between a corporation's desired strategic objectives and its realised strategic objectives or, put simply, the link between purpose and outcomes will become obscured over time – unless checked. Practitioners could conclude in fact that in many cases,

> *an organisation's strategy has not only drifted away from its purpose; it has also become disconnected from the reality of the external environment entirely.*

Evolving a reconciliation of Strategic Alignment

An assessment of the management of Strategic Alignment represents the completion of our review of the strategy system that is contained within the Third Wave Strategy framework. An illustration of the key factors of the relevance of Alignment to the Third Wave Strategy framework is presented in Figure 5.1. Content contained here is demonstrative of early research into the notion of Alignment. It was conducted by Alfred Chandler (1962) and reported in his book *Strategy and Structure*. It is embellished and redefined as follows:

> *Strategy follows purpose, structure follows strategy, systems follow structure, operations follow systems.*

It is in this context that a map of the sequence of *purpose, strategy, structure* and *operations* as a basis for Alignment within the construct of the Third Wave Strategy framework can be developed. The process is illustrated against the backdrop of the framework presented in Figure 1.1, it is highlighted in Figure 5.1.

   An understanding of just where and in what areas alignment is or isn't connected is hard to achieve. That is because points of alignment and misalignment aren't readily recognised.

Identifying areas of Alignment within the context of external vs. internal 'touch points'

We explore the strategic consequences of alignment or misalignment through the conceptualisation of the various 'plausible' touch points that relate to the three levels of 'influence' first identified in Chapter 1. As a reminder, they are:

Level 1: Outside In, external indirect environment: Universally focused environmental scanning
Level 2: Outside In, external, direct environment: Industry- and market-level analysis
Level 3: Inside Out, internal environment: Resource and core competence analysis

None of the nominated Alignment touch points that are apparent within the Third Wave Strategy framework are meant to be exclusive or conclusive, nor are they designated as official areas of Alignment in themselves. An appreciation of their existence will, however, provide you with useful insight. In critical

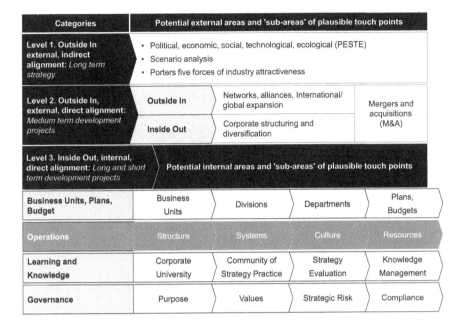

Figure 5.2 A depiction of the potential areas where plausible alignment touch points may be found

instances, an appreciation of their existence will alert you to the need to include them in some form of monitoring system. Examples of the three levels of plausible touch points are illustrated in Figure 5.2.

Level 1: Outside In, external indirect Alignment (many to many)

One of the predominant strategy tools of value at this level of Alignment is the environmental scanning protocol of PESTE analysis. This was a key contributor to the conduct of the scenario analysis which was developed in the T-wI, SPPD case study in Chapter 1. PESTE analysis provides an assessment and identification of the adverse or otherwise external forces of uncertainty that are likely to impact the future of a business. Examples of observations concerning an analysis of the PESTE forces impacting T-wI, SPPD (now PSD – Health) are listed in Case example 1.2. These were the key issues that were considered for inclusion in the 'axis of uncertainty' (Figure 1.3). The axis of uncertainty laid the foundation for the conduct of ongoing scenario analysis at PSD – Health.

A practical example of a Level 1 Third Wave Strategy Alignment touch point is global energy company Shell. An overview of its manoeuvring in this space is presented as Case example 5.2. It describes the way in which the interaction between the emerging energy division within Shell has elected to interact with the broader external environment through the introduction of an evolving transformation of the entire company.

Case example 5.2: A new lens on the future at Shell: a shift in the relationship between an organisation and its environment

As identified on their website (Shell, 2020), Shell is a "global group of energy and petrochemical companies with an average of 86,000 employees in more than 70 countries". The future of energy, its impact on our environment (especially the influence of carbon emissions) and the economy is of vital interest to Shell. Confronting the reality and immediacy of their conclusion that fossil fuels have no place in a future global community, Shell deployed its well-honed scenario planning skills as long ago as 2013 to provoke conversations about what the future of energy 'might be'. Perhaps more importantly, Shell was also keen to understand what the increasingly inevitable transformation journey might look like. Through an exploration of the world 50 to 100 years hence, the Shell strategy team evolved two possible future scenarios. As published on their website, the names for the scenarios were Mountains and Oceans. Each were used to "explore the implications of the pace of global economic development, the types of energy that will be used to power lives and the growth in greenhouse gas emissions". "These scenarios", Shell CEO of the day Peter Voser suggested, "explores complexity and asks searching questions about how we create a more reflective, responsive, and resilient business. Sharing them and driving a debate around the issues they consider are an important part of that process".

Fast forward to 2020 and Shell's scenario-focused strategic conversations have led them to the decision to transform the entire business into an electricity dominated company by 2030. Shell has taken the decision to make a 'big bet' move into global energy supplies based on an inevitability that electricity will be *the* main source of energy in the future. Their reasoning is based on their observations that: 1) improvements in storage (battery) capacities and transportability will continue to evolve, and 2) the fact that there is a growing capacity for renewables to replace fossil fuel sources of electricity generation – across the board.

Armed with an in-depth insight based on discussions around Shell's future scenarios, Maarten Wetselaar, Shell integrated gas and new energies director, was at ease in his announcement of the decision which he made at the Cambridge Energy Research Associates (CERA) Conference in Houston, Texas, in 2019 (CERAWeek, 2019). "The future of transport fuels will show a new and evolving balance between different fuels, traditional and new, depending on customers' needs and local availability" (Shell, 2019).

In his speech listed on the Shell website, Wetselaar observed that, consistent with the alternatives offered from their scenario analysis,

> the world needs many different energy solutions if it wants to achieve the goals of the Paris Agreement. We should not see this as a new rivalry to establish one single solution, but a new and evolving balance between different fuels depending on customers' needs and local availability. This is why Shell is investing in electric car charging, for example with the acquisition of charging company Greenlots here in the USA in January 2019.

In subsequent discussions with the *Financial Times*, Wetselaar observed that he was confident that Shell could readily evolve an electric power business that would equal the size of its historical oil and gas operations. "With our brand, our global presence. . . and the adjacency to our gas business – we can get our hands on the cheapest gas anywhere". Further, he noted, "If Shell achieved its goal for cutting its greenhouse gas emissions by 2035, the amount of power – of clean power – we will need to be selling . . . will make us by far the biggest power company in the world".

After further prompting from *Financial Times* journalists Crooks and Raval (2019), Wetselaar observed that many of their competitors would be at a disadvantage to them, primarily because they suffer from the overhang of legacy positions that include coal and nuclear plants. Similarly, he suggested they are held back by their centralised (Inside Out) synergistic corporate structuring and their reliance on outdated business models. Shell, on the other hand, has adopted a different (Outside In) perspective. Shell, Wetselaar noted, "sees the future customer group being much more decentralised, where people do have a battery in their basement, people do have solar panels on their roof, and they want (organisations like Shell) to help them optimise such resources".

In effect, Shell is building an Integrated Value System. As the first step in establishing a Core Competence Platform, Shell has already made a number of small acquisitions in electricity-related industries. These include the acquisition of German battery company Sonnen, the UK-based power supplier First Utility and one of Europe's largest electric vehicle charging enterprises, New Motion. It also includes the purchase in Australia of energy retailer ERM Power.

At the same time, Shell is establishing a Dynamic Market System. Based on an Outside In focused approach to market capture, Shell is planning to outperform competitors by providing a better customer experience than them. When supported by the deployment of advanced technologies, such as analytics and customer usage and optimisation patterns (to provide them with service), the bones of an Integrated Value System will be well in place.

The story told by Shell was of great interest to Alicia and her team at PSD – Health. It is a story of generational transformation; it is about an organisation that is evolving from a supplier of coal, oil and gas commodities to an energy-focused "production and supply, integrated value system in the form of orchestrator, operator and manager". It is a story that the PSD – Health leadership team could relate to very closely. It is the story of an ambidextrous journey that will see Shell slowly evolve out of its fossil fuel businesses into an integrated, renewable energy powerhouse. It is also a classic case of diversification – one that is driven by need and supported by its existing global presence and organisation structure. Finally, it is a story that exemplifies the maintenance of Long Term Strategy and its implementation in the short term, albeit one that will likely unfold over a long period of time.

Although highly motivating for the PSD – Health leadership, it also raised a red flag for Alicia and her team. It was clear to them that the Shell leadership team knew exactly where they were going and what they wanted to become. PSD – Health, on the other hand, had a good idea of what they didn't want to be but were a little fuzzy still about the detail. Their primary cause for concern was the fact that there was so much opportunity on offer from the emerging digital technology that they needed to do a lot more research to understand which way they should go next. They found some solace from the fact that the purpose of the Pathway 2 pioneering program was to define just that. Even so, they resolved that a much clearer starting point – and definition of the outcome from their current strategising – should be defined sooner rather than later.

In particular, they were conscious of the underlying principle that lay behind the articulation of the SMI Pathway of Transformation (Figure 4.2). That was the observation that was stated previously (Chapter 2) as "an organisation that enters a program of transformation *and* renewal with a clear sense of purpose is far more likely to move on to a (Phase 4) program of regeneration than those that don't" (Hunter, 2001).

Level 2: Outside In, external direct Alignment (many to one)

The Shell transformation journey has started, but at the end of the day, its completion will be subject to strategic choices enacted within a context referred to as midterm strategy. As demonstrated also in Figure 5.2, a corporation's interaction and continued Alignment with the external environment will take place from both an Outside In and Inside Out perspective (or both in the case of a merger and acquisition). Either will inevitably be components of a corporation's midterm strategy, so-called because analysis and implementation will take longer to conclude than the typical Short Term Strategy but not as long as the content contained in Long Term Strategy.

The specific action that is evolved as an outcome from a midterm strategy will also take a little while to complete. An acquisition, for example, takes a long time to identify, confirm, negotiate and finalise. A conversation piece on this conundrum is Opel, the German-based subsidiary of the US automotive company General Motors (GM). It is explored in Case example 5.3. Not only is it a good example of a Level 2 misalignment, but it also provides insight into an internal Level 3 lack of alignment.

Case example 5.3: Aligning business unit and corporate strategy at Opel Australia

Few identified a lack of alignment with US-based GM's corporate strategy following the launch of Opel in Australia in 2013. Apparently buoyed by a newfound sense of confidence following its parent company's recent emergence from Chapter 11 bankruptcy, GM's German division, Opel, sought the opportunity for expansion and chose Australia as an ideal place to establish a new distribution network. Their decision, however, was surprising. GM already had a long established market presence in that country operating under the banner of General Motors-Holden. Holden had struggled for years to maintain profitability and as a part of that had long pursued an ambition to export its products beyond its domestic markets of Australia, New Zealand and the nearby Pacific islands.

In quick order, Opel established an operations centre and national supply chain on the Australian continent. With a view to establishing a long term future in Australia, Opel established and stocked a dealership network in direct competition to all other car companies, including Holden. All this occurred while Holden continued to import Opel cars under the Holden brand, which it had been doing anyway for quite some time (Pincott, 2013).

According to Beissmann (2013), the decision makers at Opel who were involved in the scheme had made some incorrect assumptions regarding the price point at which the Opel car range could effectively compete, at least in the categories in which it chose to enter the Australian market. Volkswagen's Golf, for example, was selling well and at a reasonable discount to Opel's Astra.

After 12 months in business, reality hit home. Opel announced that the small volumes of car sales that they now expected would not deliver enough profit to sustain their viability. The business was quickly shut down and compensation agreements reached with all dealerships that had taken up their offer of distribution.

The GM Corporation has always operated as a manager of a portfolio of brands, each with a presumably free rein to take control of their own destiny. At the time that Opel was seeking to establish itself in Australia, examples of other brands owned by GM included Chevrolet, Buick, Cadillac and Vauxhall (UK). To the outsider, the experiences of Opel in its aborted expansion into Australia would appear to be baffling. On the surface, their actions demonstrated a clear lack of alignment at the Level 2 industry and market levels, even though they had access to the experiences of one of the first automotive companies to be established in the Australian market through its acquisition of local Australian car manufacturer Holden in 1931. Beyond this, there also seems to be a break down at the Level 3 corporate and division/business unit touch points of alignment. This was a situation where two already struggling divisions of GM were collaborating successfully but were allowed to compete against each other. At that time, there was no obvious immediate advantage to the corporation, which came at a time in GM's history when time really was of the essence. Setting up an automotive distribution network is no small investment, no matter how big or small the investor. Internally there would, no doubt, have been considerable and justifiable analysis and review. No matter the circumstances, the Opel case is illustrative of the way in which prevailing areas of alignment could, in fact, end up as a misalignment.

Level 3: Inside Out, internal Alignment (one to one)

A number of illustrative Level 3 Inside Out, internal Alignment touch points have been presented this book, the basis of which is again demonstrated in Figure 5.2. A fundamental and timeless issue of Alignment at this level is the challenge of strategy formulation and implementation. From an organisational perspective, it is the time-honoured challenge of aligning organisation structure with strategy. A practical example of a similar issue – the alignment of organisational purpose with division/department or business unit strategy – is demonstrated in Case example 5.4.

Case example 5.4: The investment decision: an internal departmental battle to win the right to an organisation's scarce resources

When seeking approval to expand internally, a corporation will experience internal ructions that would be apparent to those not close to the decision making process. Take a capital expenditure proposal to invest in a brand-new specialty manufacturing plant as an add-on to an existing high-volume commodity production line as an example. The manufacturing department looks to optimise plant utilisation and fixed cost absorption via the production of high-volume, noncomplex, low-optioned products. Although supportive of advanced manufacturing capabilities, such as just-in-time, agile, robotics and artificial intelligence, the underlying preference is still to keep the entire process to as fewer products as possible. The objective is to operate high-volume production runs for the purpose of absorbing high cost overheads while also keeping finished goods inventory holdings to a minimum.

In direct contrast to production, the accounting department focuses on a strategy to optimise cash flow. It sets its objectives on having zero inventory holdings, zero discounts and five-year investment cycles in the lowest priced machinery. Although supportive of the introduction of innovative, high-priced and new products it is intolerant of added features or unnecessary componentry that will increase costs unnecessarily. For them, nothing is 'strategic' if it does not meet the predetermined, board approved internal rate of return.

In direct contrast, to production and accounting the sales department seeks to optimise sales volumes through the use of large discounts, continual updates of the product range and inclusion of as many new features and benefits as possible. These are typically the short-run, complex products that demand big bet investments in new technologically advanced plant and equipment and low-volume production runs.

Finally, the human resources department is careful to ensure that morale, productivity, attendance and retention remains high. Accordingly, they must ensure as a starting point that there are no accidents, strikes, incidences of bullying, victimisation or discrimination. The best way to achieve all of these outcomes is to provide incentives to staff, one of which is higher remuneration. As these 'needs' are increasingly becoming a secondary issue as career expectations, sustainability, social responsibility and flexible work times are now assuming a higher level of importance. As technology standards increase, the demand for scarce skilled resources also increases. Working with an ever-decreasing budget is now an enduring balancing act.

Ultimately, the combined effect is probably the defining factor in the organisation's success. Finding and agreeing the right level of alignment between each makes for a tough challenge for the person preparing the capital expenditure request.

Alignment within the context of strategy practice

In our discussion in this fieldbook so far, our attention has focused mostly on Alignment of strategy content. It is, also appropriate and helpful to review the issue of Alignment in the context of strategy practice. A demonstration of a lack of alignment in strategy theory is provided by Meyer (2007). The concept that is the mainstay of Meyer's thesis is that an overwhelming majority of strategy theory exists in a state of synthesis. A synthesis, he suggests, is the situation where a decision cannot be reached without having to assess the consequential outcomes from two or more alternatives (a dilemma). Resolution of a dilemma, according to Meyer, is reached by striking a balance between a series of innovative reconciliations (a synthesis); resolution should lead to 'best of both world' solutions.

By this, Meyer (2007) is suggesting that for a number of perspectives of strategy theory, there is another equally recognised view that is the polar opposite of the other. Presented as 'dichotomies' of strategy theory, Meyer observes that tensions exist between the two extremes that make up the dichotomy. This circumstance, Meyer thought, is the same as that of a paradox – that is, the situation where there are two equally correct but opposing views of a theory that can exist at the same time. In treating the theory of strategy as a paradox, Meyer proposed that the strategy practitioner evolves a 'best of both worlds' approach when evaluating which option is the most relevant for their purpose.

An example of such a paradox in the context of a theory of strategy is that of revolutionary vs. evolutionary change. Both are valid strategic options in terms of rate of change, but it is not possible to do both at the same time. One senior executive who participated in our coursework provided us with insight into this dilemma. When referring to the introduction of advanced manufacturing capabilities in the manufacturing operation under his control, he suggested, "Although we regularly introduce changes that are revolutionary in the long term, we do it slowly; that is at an evolutionary pace". Another example is one we have referred to frequently in this book is that of an Inside Out vs. an Outside In perspective of strategy. When seeking a 'best of both worlds solution' to ease the strategic tensions that exist between each of these opposing views, we developed the SMI Model of Strategic Equilibrium (Figure 3.1) as a basis upon which a balance can be found.

Meyer (2007) proposed that strategy practitioners engage in an activity of dialectical enquiry when they seek to resolve the tensions between each opposing view. He defined dialectical enquiry as "using two opposing views (dichotomies) to arrive at a better understanding of the issue to achieve a higher level of resolution between one view, the thesis and its opposite, the antithesis (a synthesis)". A synthesis is a trade-off that can be found somewhere between one view of the truth (a thesis) and another opposite, but equally correct, version of the truth (an antithesis), as demonstrated in Figure 5.3.

When addressing the issue of Strategic Alignment in particular, it is also appropriate to wonder, "What if the application of this theory to practice misses the point"? What would happen, for example, if one strategy practitioner sought to introduce a program of rapid revolutionary change while her colleague from another department sought to introduce slow evolutionary change at the same time? It can be concluded quite justifiably, that there is just as much a need for alignment in the conduct of strategic thinking as there is in its physical implementation. To provide you with further challenges, four specific examples of dichotomies and associated tensions that have evolved from Meyer's work are presented in Figure 5.4.

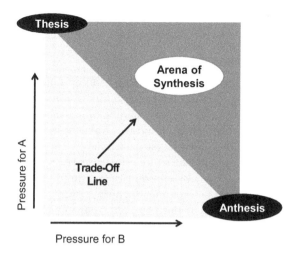

Figure 5.3 Identifying a best of both world solution at the point of synthesis that lies somewhere between a thesis and an antithesis

Strategy Topics	Strategy Dichotomies		Tensions	Examples
Corporate structure	BU specific customer focus	Corporate level resource base	Business portfolio vs. Integrated whole	General Motors vs Toyota
Network partnering	Work alone (competition)	Work together (cooperation)	Independent vs. Integrated	Apple vs. Microsoft
International	Globalisation	Localisation	Global uniformity vs. International diversity	Toyota vs. HSBC
Organising	Top-down control	Bottom-up 'chaos'	Bureaucracy vs. Choice	Navy vs. Pirates

Figure 5.4 Illustrative dichotomies, associated strategic tensions and illustrative examples

Managing the dichotomies of strategy in practice and at T-wI, PSD – Health

We explore the content of each dichotomy presented in Figure 5.4 next, and its impact within the boundaries of our case study company: PSD – Health.

Corporate structuring

The notion of corporate structuring was introduced in Chapter 2 where reference was made to the challenge for the corporation to decide between a posture of industry leadership or followership. Our reference to corporate structuring here, seeks to address the choices between those of the optimisation of customer relations versus those of resource utilisation. The former points to a preference for the optimisation of a decentralised high-cost business unit structure. The latter points to a preference for the realisation of synergistic, centralised, lower-cost corporate structure:

- The first is a structure that is decentralised and optimises customer service through a portfolio of customer-facing business units. An example is GM (refer to the Opel case study, Case example 5.3). Each division or business unit of GM is an independent brand that operates its own manufacturing facilities and supplies its own target markets.
- The second is a centralised structure – one that is designed to optimise its resource base (lowest cost) by consolidating common fixed cost overheads (some of which would be customer-focused anyway) in a centralised location. An example of this is the German car manufacturer BMW, which operates manufacturing plants in a few locations throughout the world and presents the same model range sourced from a single or few but dedicated manufacturing facilities that supply customers in every part of the world.

For years PSD – Health has been locked into a corporate structure that barely had the customer in mind. Now mindful of the need to define either an Inside Out or Outside In construct, Alicia Manning asked Charles Bakersfield to ensure that the customer focus was a key priority for them from now on.

Network partnering

It took the reappointment of Steve Jobs to the role of CEO to save Apple from extinction in 1997. Still a staunchly independent industry participant, Apple has for years benefitted from its Integrated Value System approach to structuring. In the operation of this system, Apple integrates its Core Competence Platform with a number of Dynamic Market Systems. Each are presented in the form of a range of integrated hardware, software and app products that include Apple TV, Apple Watch, iPhone and iCloud. Apple is recognised as one of the most independent and successful companies in history. The primary competitor to Apple, Microsoft, on the other hand, has no qualms about partnering with others if the end game is likely to be bigger and better than going it alone. Whereas Apple hardware, for example, is designed to suit Apple software as a priority, Microsoft software is designed to be installed on numerous machines. The tensions that prevail between the strategic option of working as a lone competitor versus that of an open, cooperative network are stark – and will vary depending on the circumstances of each business.

How does a business get a 'best of both worlds' answer to networking? As an example of an organisation that wanted to emulate the Apple ecosystem format but failed is the UK-based Thomas Cook Travel company. Commencing business as a travel booking agency, this company needed minimal investment in capital equipment. When operating in the form of an agency only, it carried minimal risk. Fast forward to late 2019, and Thomas Cook has collapsed while carrying a much higher risk when acting as an independent travel agent, as well as a tour operator and owner of a non-integrated and independent airline. Airlines typically require 100% utilisation all year round if they are to maintain a sufficient cash flow to ensure a balanced budget from their capital intensive aeroplanes. Thomas Cook did not have the means to fulfil such a cash flow, as it suffered low volumes in the cold European winters. Had it chosen to partner with an existing airline rather than buy one, its original 'balance' would more likely have been maintained. Instead, it succumbed to the inevitable as it entered an irreversible bankruptcy in September 2019.

As PSD – Health is a traditional 'go it alone' and highly independent kind of business, Alicia was determined that this relatively unheard of aspect of corporate structuring would not go missing from the PSD – Health radar. She thought it appropriate, therefore, to include the observation in her next discussion with Charles and her team. In particular, she was concerned that their combined lack of understanding of advanced digitised technology should not lead them into a dark place. Although a business case and rationale would be required, Alicia was prepared to take any partnering proposal to Jenny Wong and the corporate office if necessary.

International strategy

For years, it was expected that in order to 'go global', a company first had to build a local (home) presence and core business from which an international (a few international countries) and then global (many countries) empire could evolve. Today, web-enabled online trading allows an organisation to start global – and stay that way. This is, of course, a general rule; there are many constraints and barriers to such an approach. As an existing resource-rich company, Toyota is in a strong position to maintain its global presence where it sells the same range of products (with some minor variations) in every country in the world. HSBC Bank, on the other hand, has an international presence but must tailor this advantage to the local legislative constraints of each country, the constraints of its information and management systems and the demands of its customers. An obvious example of the latter is the Islamist requirement that no interest is charged for lending money. This is a big challenge for banks that do not have a strong Islamist presence in the country of their origin.

The application of this international challenge to PSD – Health was a conundrum for Alicia. Much of their services would require local representation, not because of customer demand but more because of the local supply network that requires close relationships, a high level of trust and extreme secrecy about many of its product features. The groundwork for the management of these issues had been established but not to the extent that a dramatic elevation in a global presence would allow. Alicia saw this as a key priority for inclusion in their strategy deployment and advised Charles and her team that she would seek divisional- and corporate-level support and resources in its resolution.

Organising

One of the greatest transformations in attitudes to the management and leadership of organisations and, indeed, society in general in recent times is the evolution from a Dickensian model of dictatorship to one of engagement and openness. In some organisations, the nature of the entity requires a continued degree of bureaucracy – or so it seems. Navies, police, armies and banks are examples of organisations in which a degree of authoritative control is mandated. In contrast, partnerships, creative consulting agencies and universities can thrive on minimal bureaucracy and even chaos.

Alicia had never envisioned a state of chaos emerging at PSD – Health. She was, though, keen to introduce a greater degree of freedom and creative spirit. She was particularly keen also to encourage an open strategy practice in PSD – Health, as was her boss, Jenny Wong. It wasn't until the risk of chaos was suggested that her attention was turned to the reality of allowing a bottom-up form of organisation leadership to emerge. As a leader committed to a philosophy of free spirit (pirate) over command and control (navy), she asked for time out while she considered her options. Seeking a synthesis would require a lot of thought. Perhaps, she contemplated, she could find some boundaries upon which resolution could be found. Not one to dwell on reflection and pontification for too long, Alicia convened a special COSP working party to apply an agile principled working team to identify and define a solution. It was a little ironic, she thought: a natural inclination to apply a 'chaos'-based approach to the resolution of the practice of chaos.

In seeking alignment, the team resolved a best of both worlds solution would be to maintain the philosophy of free-thinking chaos but in a format of 'agile'-oriented boundaries and conditions. An orientation of 'chaos' would be encouraged in most areas. In areas where strong financial control, regulatory compliance and the need for elevated levels of risk management prevailed, she would be less likely to encourage too much pirate behaviour over the constraints of the navy. We incorporate the issue of Alignment – or lack thereof – in an external and internal context in our following catch up with the T-wI, PSD – Health case study review.

Revisiting the optimisation of Strategic Alignment at PSD – Health

The notion of Strategic Alignment in the eyes of Charles and his team had suddenly taken centre stage. As with most organisations in recent times, the skills required to rationalise PSD – Health's core business were well practised and well understood. Even as a reengineering, restructuring and supply chain redesign veteran, however, core business change leader Stephany Lee admitted she was unsure about how the Level 1 external issue of 4IR digitised technologies would impact core operations. With the approval of transformation leader Charles Bakersfield, Stephany approached Chief

Technology Officer Sanjay Barti to propose that they, Charles and Alicia talk through the issues.

A delighted Sanjay was quick to get on board. So important was the need for alignment with SPPD strategy and future developments in digital technology he also thought it essential to get the Program of Continual Strategy Renewal (Figure 5.5) up and running as soon as possible.

Charles is a highly experienced project, program and change management leader. Although supportive of the idea of working together rather than in isolation, he was cautious about the direction that Stephany and Sanjay were taking the management of the unknown digital technology. He had warned the leadership team previously about the danger of getting caught up in the Level 1 issues of emergent technology and societal change even though it represented significant opportunity to the business. Facing extreme pressure to deliver the Level 3 task they had been assigned, there was no ambiguity about the fact that their number-one priority was to get the core business back into shape and the emerging business pilot – in aged care – up and running.

To emphasise this point, Alicia and Charles stressed in their meeting with Sanjay and Stephany that there should be no steps missed in the Level 3 internal alignment transformation program. Concerned by the fact that the program was starting to drift away from a clarity of objectives and a consciousness of alignment, Charles moved to ensure that the direction of the project had a clear intent, purpose and focus. His intention was to restore a potential loss of guidance that had once been established in the development of the Pathway of Transformation and Renewal (Figure 4.2). Although the health division Strategic Architecture was useful (Figure 3.4), it was now starting to become less relevant as aged care assumed its own direction and the two short term pathways to implementation started to move ahead of the original thinking.

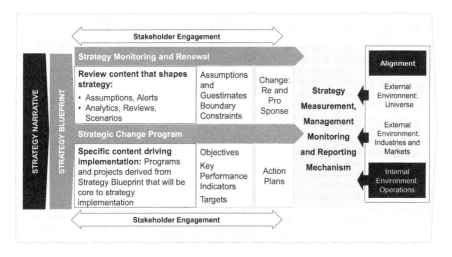

Figure 5.5 Program of Continual Strategy Renewal incorporating alignment

Accordingly, Charles called for a more precise representation of strategy of relevance to the transformation agenda to be developed and the depiction of what it was they were transforming to. Specifically, Charles, Alicia and the leadership team took the transformation program membership back to basics. In instigating this action, Charles wasn't seeking to redefine Long or Short Term Strategy; quite the contrary. All he was trying to do was provide confirmation and clarification on specific points of relevance. With the full involvement of the members of the PSD – Health COSP, an immediate move to develop an updated Strategic Architecture was instigated. Subsequent to this is an individual/independent Strategy Narrative and Strategy Blueprint for both the core (PSD – Health) and emerging business (aged care). Accordingly, a final Strategic Architecture depicting a reinvented and restructured PSD – Health, Integrated Value System is presented in Figure 5.6.

Primary objectives from the establishment of a separate core business, the Pathway 1 Strategy Blueprint, they resolved, would be to allow PSD – Health to take advantage of both *re* and *prosponsive* opportunities as they arose. It is described as follows.

Pathway 1: Agile Adaptation: Nurture and optimise core business

A revised Strategy Narrative describing a Short Term Strategy for this pathway was built around a Strategic Change Agenda of "transform to a specialised, hyper – high performance, integrated personalised service provider". The associated Strategy Blueprint is illustrated in Figure 5.7.

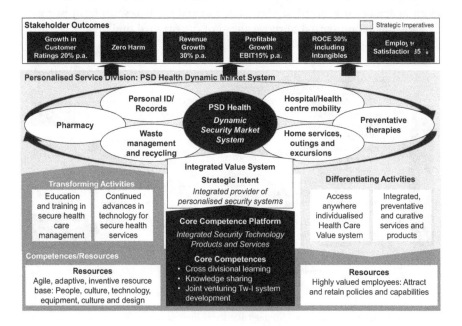

Figure 5.6 Final Strategic Architecture: reinvented and restructured – health value system

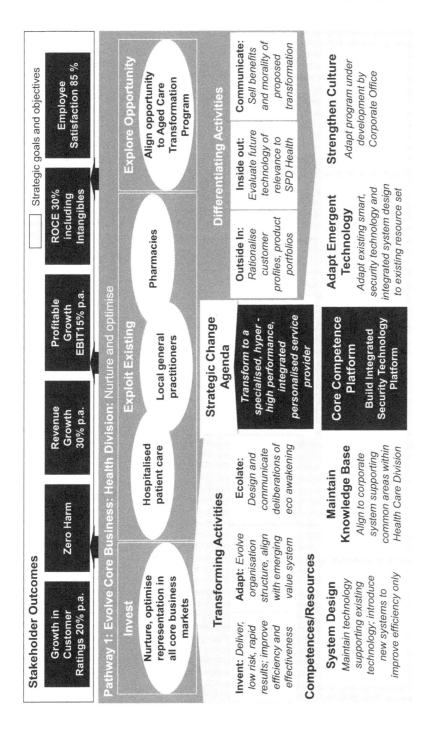

Figure 5.7 Final Strategy Blueprint Pathway 1 – core business (healthcare)

As the core and traditional business for PSD – Health, the primary content of its Strategy Narrative was reconfirmed as follows:

- Improve the efficiency and effectiveness of existing technology by cutting costs.
- Invest in technology aimed at the introduction of automation and elimination of waste in manufacturing processes, as well as back-office support.
- Satisfy consumer concerns that SPPD placed too greater a reliance on plastics.
- Satisfy growth requirements through investment in greater integration across the T-wI company infrastructure.

Most importantly, the key objective was to ensure that once the pilot transformation program that was being undertaken as Pathway 2 was completed, the two pathways to implementation would be reintegrated back to one. It was expected, however, that such an outcome would take approximately another year to complete. Reintegration of the entire PSD – Health business would move quite rapidly after that.

Pathway 2: Deliberate Disruption: **Evolve emerging business**

With the eventual reintegration of Pathways 1 and 2 in mind, the Strategy Narrative describing a revised Short Term Strategy for Pathway 2 was built around the same Strategic Change Agenda of "transform to a specialised, hyper – high performance, integrated personalised service provider". In their preparation of the Strategy Narrative for Pathway 2, a further revision of the divisional structure was deemed appropriate. Chief Technology Officer Sanjay Barti was the only member of the leadership team who worked solely for the benefit of the second pathway to implementation identified in the aged care strategy. He was accordingly very keen to have his say in the structure and content of the Strategy Blueprint. Content contained within the Strategy Narrative here was reconfirmed with Sanjay's specific approval:

- Identify, design and articulate the 'to-be' Core Competence Platform–based infrastructure supporting the newly defined Dynamic Market System. Included in this are the steps required to get to the future (based on a backcasting methodology) and a definition of the starting point for the 'to-be' Integrated Value System.

  As well as a starting point for regeneration, the 'to-be' definition of PSD – Health's value system would be representative of the handing over of the single-step transformational Strategy Implementation program to that of a Program of Continual Strategy Renewal.
- Conduct deeper research into the implications of the timing and profitability of 'smart printing', 'smart packaging' and other related but existing and proven technology.

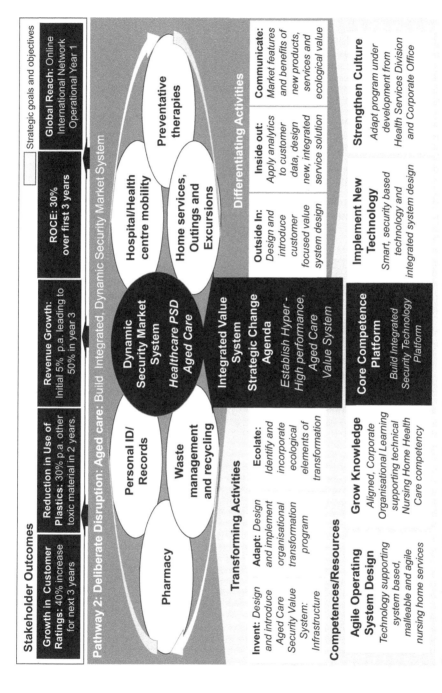

Figure 5.8 Final Strategy Blueprint Pathway 2 – emerging business (aged care pilot)

- Identify opportunities to capitalise on existing capabilities – realise quick wins.
- Identify competences required to support PSD – Health's aged care move to shape the future through the introduction of evolutionary but rapid transformation using digital technologies.

The revised Strategy Blueprint for Pathway 2 (emerging business (aged care pilot)) is demonstrated in Figure 5.8.

Comfortable with the introduction of more concise and visible control mechanisms, Charles and members of the transformation team now clearly understood what they needed to do. They quickly moved to incorporate their objectives and topics of evaluation into an appropriate, alignment-based alerting mechanism. This would be similar in construct to the alerting mechanism discussed and illustrated in Chapter 4 (Figure 4.6). This specific alerting mechanism, however, would focus primarily on the physicality of Third Wave Strategy practice – that is, its content, systems and processes.

The monitoring of alignment issues associated with internal strategising were considered to be issues of philosophy and entropy. Components of the latter content will be extracted from the kind of analysis presented in Figure 5.4. These are issues of dichotomous alignment that include the specifics of organisational structuring, network partnering, globalisation and organising. The management of these issues would, Alicia and the COSP suggested, be included in the strategy toolkit as key areas for evaluation and review. This would be complemented with their insertion in the T-wI Corporate University leadership development curriculum as well. In this form, it was considered it would provide a natural foundation upon which an alignment between organisational learning and strategy could be grounded.

6 Future strategy practice

Chapter overview

In the concluding chapter to a series of workshop-oriented programs, we seek to wrap up and conclude discussions on past topics while projecting and speculating on what the future may hold for strategy as a discipline. Our discussion is limited therefore, to two key topics. The first is an expansion of the topic of open strategy practice. It is grounded in developments found in the people and behavioural aspects of Third Wave Strategy. The second is system and process related. It is the introduction of the topic of the Green Shoot Strategy.

In our assessment and discussion around open strategy practice, we are reinforcing a trend that is impacting not only the practice of strategy but also the practice of management and leadership overall. In our introduction to Green Shoot Strategy, we are evolving the notion of Deliberate Disruption in the context of organisational transformation and a notion of accelerated Deliberate Disruption; in the context of invention of new business and potentially new industries altogether. Each provide a suitable platform for group discussion around the topic of 'next steps' in strategy and presentations of lessons learned from the foregoing content explored and discussed in this book and its companion introductory book.

Learning insights

In this chapter considerable emphasis is placed on the notion of open strategy practice in the context of Third Wave Strategy. At the moment, its practice is like a silent army moving ever forward to victory. As a non-scientific concept, its practice lies more in common sense and detailed design than in theory. Having said that, we do introduce a stepped approach to its implementation based on research conducted in one method deployed by the iconic web-based media company Wikimedia. From an analysis of their approach, it was possible to establish a similar program of relevance to our imaginary company PSD – Health. Rather conveniently, the outcome provides a foundation upon which a Green Shoot Strategy can be identified for further development at PSD – Health. Ultimately, this provides a useful basis upon which the book concludes and assessments of learning commences.

Work plan phase 6: Future Strategy Practice

As the final piece in the puzzle presented in Case example 0.1, our work plan now comes to an end through the completion of our review of open strategy practice and the topic of Green Shoot Strategy. An envisaged pathway that future strategy practice will follow, it is shown in Figure 6.1. As you will observe from that illustration, there is a trodden road map that the typical corporation will follow as it goes from early growth to decline, and inevitably a fight for survival as it fights desperately to avoid the perils of a strategic drift. An alternative pathway is available; it follows strategies of prosponsive thinking and a hoped for turnaround associated with 'thrival' as a result of active prosponsive thinking and invention.

You are invited to ask, however, what would happen if instead of a pursuit of organisational transformation a corporation could follow a pathway leading to new opportunity and new businesses, markets and industries altogether. The question is addressed in the context of Green Shoot Strategy next, along with a perspective of open strategy as future aspects of strategy practice are explored further.

Introduction: future strategy practice

Fundamental to the future of strategy is the inevitability that its practice will become increasingly open to all stakeholders from the perspectives of both formulation and implementation. As suggested previously in this and its companion book, *Corporate Strategy (Remastered) I*, the idea of open strategy practice is a phenomenon that "affords actors greater strategic transparency and/or inclusion" (Hautz, 2017). We commence our discussion in this chapter on the

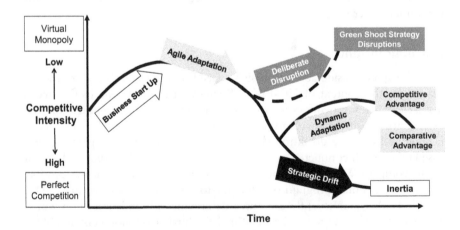

Figure 6.1 Life cycles of businesses engaging in the four perspectives of sponsive strategic change

topic of open strategy practice and maintain this as a philosophy throughout this chapter and into the future.

Open strategy practice in play

To provide insight into methods of practice, provided in Case example 6.1 is a summary of findings from Heracleous et al. (2019), based on their research into the experiences of Wikimedia in their endeavours to introduce open strategy practice into that organisation.

Case example 6.1: Open strategy practice at Wikimedia

On its website, Wikimedia describes itself as a global movement whose mission is to bring free educational content to the world. Operator of the universal knowledge database Wikipedia, Wikimedia suggests on its website that it "strives to bring about a world in which every single human being can freely share in the sum of all knowledge" (Wikimedia, 2019). Expressing a philosophy of transparency, openness and inclusion, as well as the use of "the wisdom of the crowd", has not only become part of its DNA but is also integral to its adoption of open strategy.

As an outcome of empirical research conducted by Heracleous et al. (2019), a four-step method of the open strategy practice was identified. We apply their methodology to Third Wave Strategy as follows:

  Level setting: In this introductory step, Heracleous et al. (2019) noted that Wikimedia created a knowledge database that described its open approach to strategy in order to provide prospective participants with insight into its practice. In their communication about the program, Wikimedia invited people to express their views by participating in a survey designed to collect suggestions about strategic issues of relevance to Wikimedia. The responses were reviewed and analysed. They were then filtered down to three key issues that addressed the topics of "sustainability, development and accessibility" (Heracleous et al. (2019).

  Deep dives: Further review of these three issues were handed out to members of various task forces. Each were given the responsibility of refining content. Although a non-open process, Heracleous et al. (2019) observed, "Decision-making powers were allocated to one person for each task force". Each task force was then given the responsibility of distilling submissions into key areas of interest. They would then require further processing to be undertaken in the next step.

Synthesis: The deep dives that were selected for further review were then passed on for final processing, with the key source of prioritisation being the extent to which recommendations would be feasible or not.

Call to action: As described by Heracleous et al. (2019) the entire Wikimedia 'open community' that was engaged in the process was then called on to comment further and refine the conclusions reached in the first report. It contained five strategic priorities: "quality content, innovation, increasing participation, growing readership and stabilising infrastructure. Each were considered to be clear, specific, aligned and implementable". From there, a 'call to action' was issued with a commitment to, and celebration of, a decree to proceed to implementation.

While clearly an objective to develop a Short Term Strategy satisfying short term needs in Wikimedia, the method deployed does provide a foundation upon which a more comprehensive open strategy system could be based. What it doesn't do, though, is identify reasons why an organisation wouldn't engage in an open strategy practice in the first place. Insight into this situation is provided by Hautz et al. (2017), who observed that in the face of the many obvious advantages, an open strategy practice can result in a number of negative outcomes that could arise as well. As an example, Hautz et al. (2017) observed that although the provision of access to wider sources of knowledge is useful, this very act can result in a reduction in "speed, flexibility and control" of the strategising process. Similarly, although engagement and openness improve a commitment to the strategy process, that commitment can also be undermined should the expectations about the impact of a contribution be misconstrued or ignored.

Perhaps most importantly, there is an ever-present fear amongst strategy practitioners that an open disclosure of confidential information about firm-specific strategy will lead to a threat to a firm's competitiveness. It is our observation, however, that in most cases, there is only a small percent of strategy that can't be observed from afar and can be legitimately classified as confidential.

Open strategy practice at PSD – Health

After some two years into PSD – Health's transformation, the two pathways of Strategy Implementation had become one. The implementation of core business profitability had recovered and was starting to show strong signs of profitable growth. At the same time, the reinvention of aged care now involved a lot of major projects. These included the trialling of artificial intelligence in the tracking and tamper-proofing of drugs and certificates. Artificial intelligence was also applied to the system used to monitor patient drug management in the issuing of scripts and dosage control. Blockchain was seen as a key enabler of many of their services, and a trial was underway to explore future developments and possibilities with that capability. All progress was being continually tracked and monitored within the corporate-funded, intranet-embedded PSD – Health strategy monitoring dashboard.

T-wI Corporate University had now been established, and PSD – Health's strategy, learning and COSP all fell under its umbrella. The key focus of both Alicia's and Jenny's attention was to get a pilot Green Shoot Strategy, accelerated Deliberate Disruption program up and running. The combination of both, they thought, would provide an ideal subject for experimentation. In setting this up, Alicia asked Charles to take new recruit Francesca Jones under his wing to formulate an approach.

Consistent with the objective of combining an agile open strategy practice with a Green Shoot Strategy deliberation, Charles and Francesca met to develop a work plan. Key parties to the exercise would be T-wI Corporate University, the COSP and the PSD – Health leadership team. The methodology deployed was similar to that adopted by Wikimedia.

Conduct of a pilot open and Green Shoot Strategy program

The project as defined was designed to be undertaken in four steps. They are described as follows.

1 **Project communications:** The first task Charles and Francesca identified was to communicate the projects objectives, the methodology to be deployed and a request for suggestions as to the potential areas where opportunities may be found. Accordingly, an explanation and description of the notion of Green Shoot Strategy was issued on the T-wI, PSD – Health intranet. At the same time, a description of the proposed project was provided, along with a submission form that could be completed by those with ideas for review. An email campaign was also launched that provided the same information, with the idea being to make the invitation more personal. The use of social media was also explored; it included an analysis of the value offered from various applications that included Facebook, Wikimedia, Instagram, Slack and blogs.

2 **Opportunity assessment and evaluation:** Charles and Francesca were pleased with the size of the first response. Some 200 submissions were received, of which 50 were viable and ten offered significant promise. Following further review of those ten, only one really stood out. It was a proposal from a team of COSP members, each of whom had been closely involved in the aged care digitisation program. This was selected

unanimously by the Green Shoot Strategy pilot leadership team for trialling and investment, if proved to be warranted.

Alicia was extremely careful in this selection process not to ignore the effort
and commitment of those who had taken the time to submit a proposal.
Accordingly, she contacted each person individually via email, thanking them
for their efforts and encouraging them to resubmit in subsequent rounds.

3   **Details of the first Green Shoot Strategy opportunity:** Having been
exposed to the benefits that could be derived from the digitisation of the aged
care business, the implementation team had spotted an opportunity that was
not specifically 'on strategy' for PSD – Health in its current format. It could,
though, be suitable for a new division should it be proved to be viable. The
digitalisation of aged care was well underway, and some members had concluded that the technology that was available would be extremely beneficial to
some extent in its current format and to a greater extent in future applications
beyond the immediate strategic boundaries of PSD – Health. There was scope
however to add value to PSD should a separate business unit be established.

4   **The Green Shoot Strategy proposal:** In introducing the PSD – Health
solution to its customers, the aged care team had observed that although
the reaction had been positive, it was still extremely hard to sell the vision
and the promise (as opposed to its realisation) of higher quality, lower cost
and far more extensive systems-based, service solutions. Rather than simply
providing a service to aged care, why not, they thought, enter the entire
aged care business on their own? They didn't need to buy nursing homes,
community housing villages, fitness centres, hospitals or even medical sur-
geries to do this, although they could if they wanted to. Either way, it was
thought, PSD – Health Aged Care Services (as they referred to themselves
now) could provide a core business that coordinated all of the above in
every community that required such a service to be provided. Building on
a Core Competence Platform of retirement village management, aged care
management, Blockchain empowered, secure document printing and packaging and health management (prevention and treatment), the aged care
team saw a business opportunity that had a natural Dynamic Market System
in place.

The construct of the Dynamic Market System included social entertainment and education programs, health treatment and health management
programs. These included aged care specialist services of chiropody, physi-
otherapy, hydrotherapy and a range of other health services. These additional
services could include personal financial management, mobility management
and dietary management. A membership accommodation program could
also be established, tailored to in-house, full-time guests, short term guests,
day-care guests and visitors. Operated on a subscription basis, members could
live at home and still be included in all the social, health and other personal
management programs. They could also participate on an as needed basis and
as short term guests. For those not living in a facility, a guarantee could be
made that a place would be found for them when the right time came.

A proposal for this program was developed by Charles and Francesca and distributed for review. It was accepted overwhelmingly; the development of a full-blown business case was commenced. From here, the PSD – Health business went from strength to strength and are well on their way to becoming a Hyper – HPO.

Next steps

In our conclusion to this fieldbook, we invite you to prepare a presentation or report addressing a business situation of the strategy of your choice. A sample question you may care to address is included in the Appendix.

Appendix

Example case study to be used in coursework or consultant-led strategy development program

Subject: a future Amazon: transforming the *everything store* into the *everywhere store*

When CEO and founder Jeff Bezos established Amazon in 1994, his ambition was to establish an online shopping facility that would sell anything and everything. Starting out as an online book seller, Bezos's 'everything store' is now a global phenomenon that would be better considered as an 'everywhere store'. Representative of a Hyper – High Performance Organisation (HPO), one arm of Amazon's 'everywhere' presence is its electronic communications capability, of which its Echo and Dot (Alexa) gadgets play a central role. Amazon is reported to have sold over 100 million Alexa's since its launch.

From our review of the Amazon success story in our companion book, *Corporate Strategy (Remastered) I*, it was concluded that essentially Amazon is an example of an operational, Integrated Value System. In its strategy and structure, Amazon effectively leverages a Core Competence Platform that consists of a lean and agile, technology-enabled supply chain into a Dynamic Market System. The market system is represented by a network of related service offerings centred around the physical technology of Amazon Prime. Everything Amazon does is wrapped in an overriding culture of passionate customer centricity.

Issue to be addressed

Amazon benefits from 1) its possession of a Core Competence Platform, 2) its obsession with a customer-first focus and 3) its application of enabling technology (in particular Amazon Prime) as a key component of its Dynamic Market System. In making it the *everywhere store* (Oremus, 2019), its (albeit hidden) ambition is to have Alexa devices installed in every house and office in the world. The essence of Alexa in this format is its capability with the Internet of Everything (i-scoop, 2020) applications that incorporate artificial intelligence and deep-dive data analytics. These in turn are deployed to answer random questions via Internet searches, turn lights on and off (remotely), program household appliances from an (autonomous) car, organise calendars via smartphones and so on.

Question to be answered

What would you do to lead Amazon into the next century and in what areas would you recommend it should build its greatest presence? In your answer, you must deploy at least ten constructs and tools described in the Third Wave Strategy narrative and justify your answer in a written report and formal presentation to your colleagues. You must include an analysis of Amazon's Core Competence Platform and Dynamic Market System, as well as its position in the SMI Model of Strategic Equilibrium. You must also prepare a draft Strategy Narrative, a Strategic Architecture and Strategy Blueprint for the Amazon of the future. Content does not have to be factual but reflective of what the future may hold for Amazon. You may work independently or as a team on this assignment.

Bibliography

Ambrosini, A., & Bowman, C. What are Dynamic Capabilities and are they a Useful Construct in Strategic Management? *International Journal of Management Reviews*, 11(1), 2009.

Amit, R., & Schoemaker, P. J. Strategic Assets and Organizational Rent. *Strategic Management Journal*, 14(1), 1993, 33–46.

Ansoff, H. I. Strategies for Diversification. *Harvard Business Review*, 35(5), September–October 1957.

Ansoff, H. I. *Corporate Strategy*. New York: McGraw-Hill, 1965.

Araya, D. 3 Things You Need to Know About Augmented Intelligence. *Forbes*, January 22, 2019, www.forbes.com/sites/danielaraya/2019/01/22/3-things-you-need-to-know-about-augmented-intelligence/#4a26c2923fdc.

Baghai, M., Coley, S., & White, D. *The Alchemy of Growth*. New York: Perseus Publishing, 1999.

Biessmann, T. Opel Australia Closure: How it Happened and where to from Here. *Caradvice*, August 8, 2013, www.caradvice.com.au/245654/opel-australia-closure-how-it-happened-and-where-to-from-here/.

Bolman, L. G., & Deal, T. *Reframing Organisations: Artistry, Choice, and Leadership*, Sixth Edition. New York: John Wiley & Sons, 2017.

Brown, T. Design Thinking. *Harvard Business Review*, June 2008, 85–92.

Cadbury, D. *Chocolate Wars: From Cadbury to Kraft – 200 Years of Sweet Success and Bitter Rivalry*. London: Harper Press, 2010.

Calof, J. L., & Wright, S. Competitive Intelligence: A Practitioner, Academic and Inter-Disciplinary Perspective. *European Journal of Marketing*, 42, 2008.

CERAWeek (Cambridge Energy Research Associates (CERA) Conference in Houston, Texas, in 2019) https://ceraweek.com/index.html.

Chakravarthy, B., & Lorange, P. *Profit or Growth? Why You Don't Have to Choose*. Harlow: Pearson Education, 2008.

Chandler, A. D. *Strategy and Structure: Chapters in the History of the Industrial Enterprise*. Cambridge, MA: MIT Press, 1962.

Courtney, H. *20/20 Foresight: Crafting Strategy in an Uncertain World*. Cambridge, MA: Harvard Business Press, 2001.

Crooks, E., Raval, A. Shell Aims to Become World's Largest Electricity Company, *Financial Times*, Houston, March 13, 2019, https://www.ft.com/content/87cfc31e-44e7-11e9-b168-96a37d002cd3.

de Geus, A. Planning as Learning. *Harvard Business Review*, March–April 1988, 70–74.

de Waal, A. A. *The Characteristics of a High Performance Organisation, Centre for Organizational Performance*. Netherlands: Maastricht School of Management, January 2010.

Encyclopaedia of American Industries, Reference for Business, Sysco, https://www.refer enceforbusiness.com/history2/10/Sysco-Corporation.html.

Flood, R. L. *Rethinking the Fifth Discipline – Learning Within the Unknowable.* New York: Rout-ledge, 1999.

Ford Motor Company – 2018 Annual Report, https://s22.q4cdn.com/857684434/files/ doc_financials/2018/annual/2018-Annual-Report.pdf.

The Foundation for Critical Thinking: Website 2019, www.criticalthinking.org/pages/ our-conception-of-critical-thinking/411.

Georgantzas, N. C., & Acar, W. *Scenario Driven Planning: Learning to Manage Strategic Uncer-tainty.* Westport, CT: Quorum Books, 1995.

Gilbert, D., & Wilson, T. Prospection: Experiencing the Future. *Science*, 317(5843), 2007, 1351–1354.

Godet, M., & Roubelat, F. Creating the Future: The Use and Misuse of Scenarios. *Long Range Planning*, 29(2), 1985, 164–171.

Golden, B. R. Research Notes. The Past is the Past – Or is it? The Use of Retrospec-tive Accounts as Indicators of Past Strategy. *Academy of Management Journal*, 35(4), 1992, 848–860.

Grant, R. M. *Contemporary Strategy Analysis and Cases: Text and Cases.* New York: John Wiley & Sons, 2016.

Hamel, G., & Prahalad, C. K. Strategy as Stretch and Leverage. *Harvard Business Review*, Bos-ton, MA, March–April 1993 Issue.

Hautz, J., Seidl, D., & Whittington, R. Open Strategy: Dimensions, Dilemmas, Dynamics, *Long Range Planning*. Elsevier Ltd., London, 2017.

Hedley, B. *Strategy and the Business Portfolio, Long Range Planning.* London, February 1977, https://www.sciencedirect.com/science/article/abs/pii/0024630177900425?via%3 Dihub.

Heracleous, L., Wawarta, C., Gonzalez, S., & Paroutis, S. How a Group of NASA Renegades Transformed Mission Control. *MIT Sloan Management Review*, Cambridge, MA, USA, Spring 2019.

Hunter, P. W. *Strategic Revitalisation: A Strategic Business Model of Innovation and Growth.* Doctor of Business Administration Thesis, Graduate School of Business and Law, RMIT Univer-sity, Melbourne, Australia, 2001.

IBM Research Website, www.research.ibm.com/5-in-5/ai-and-bias/.

i-scoop, https://www.i-scoop.eu/internet-of-things-guide/internet-of-everything/.

Jarzabkowski, P., & Spee, A. P. Strategy-as-Practice: A Review and Future Directions for the Field. *International Journal of Management Reviews*, 11(1), 2009, 69–95.

Kaplan, R., & Anderson, S. *Time-Driven Activity-Based Costing.* Boston, MA: Harvard Business Review, November 2004.

Kim, W. C., & Mauborgne, R. Value Innovation: A Leap into the Blue Ocean. *Journal of Busi-ness Strategy*, 26(4), 22–28, 2005.

Kim, C. W. and Mauborgne, R. *Blue Ocean Strategy: How To Create Uncontested Marke Space And Make Competition Irrelevant.* Boston, MA: Harvard Business Press, 2006.

Kirby, J., & Stewart, T. The Institutional Yes. *Harvard Business Review*, Cambridge, MA, Extracted by Harvard Business Review from the October 20017 issue and posted on their blog/web site at https://hbr.org/2007/10/the-institutional-yes.

Lovallo, D., & Sibony, O. The Case for Behavioural Strategy. *The McKinsey Quarterly*, 2010, www.mckinsey.com/business-functions/strategy-and-corporate-finance/our-insights/ the-case-for-behavioral-strategy.

Magretta, J. *Why Business Models Matter.* Boston, MA: Harvard Business Review 2002.

McKinsey and Company, Agile Compendium, October 2018, https://www.mckinsey. com/~/media/McKinsey/Business%20Functions/Organization/Our%20Insights/ Harnessing%20agile%20compendium/Harnessing-Agile-compendium-October-2018. ashx.

McLaughlin. M.W. *You Can't Be What You Can't See, The Power of Opportunity to Change Young Lives*. Cambridge, MA: Harvard Education Press, April 2018.

Meyer, R. J. H. *Mapping the Mind of the Strategist: A Quantitative Methodology for Measuring the Strategic Beliefs of Executives*. ERIM Ph.D. Series Research in Management. Erasmus Research Institute of Management (ERIM), May 24, 2007.

Nalebuff, B. J., & Brandenburger, A. M. The Right Game: Use Game Theory to Shape Strategy. *Harvard Business Review*, 73(4), 57–71, 1995.

Oremus, W. Amazon Just Became the Everywhere Store; Alexa is Coming for your Eyes, Ears, Hands, and . . . Dog? *OneZero*, September 26, 2019, https://onezero.medium.com/ amazon-just-became-the-everywhere-store-dce9353decd3.

Pincott, K. Opel to Close Down in Australia. *Carsguide*, August 2, 2013, www.carsguide.com. au/car-news/opel-to-close-down-in-australia-22419.

Porter, M. *Competitive Strategy: Techniques for Analysing Industries and Competitors*. New York: The Free Press, 1980.

Porter, M. *Competitive Advantage: Creating and Sustaining Superior Performance*. New York: The Free Press, 1985.

Porter, M. What is Strategy? *Harvard Business Review*, November–December 1996, 61–78.

Porter, M. *Competitive Strategy: Techniques for Analysing Industries and Competitors*. New York: The Free Press, 2018.

Powell, T. H., & Angwin, D. N. The Role of the Chief Strategy Officer. *MIT Sloan Management Review*, 54(1), 2012, 15.

Prahalad, C. K., & Hamel, G. The Core Competence of the Corporation. *Harvard Business Review*, 68(3), 1990, 79–91.

Repenning, N. P., Kieffer, D., & Repenning, J. A New Approach to Designing Work, *MIT Sloan Management Review*, Winter, 2018, https://sloanreview.mit.edu/ article/a-new-approach-to-designing-work/.

Rutschman, A., & Stephen, S. Hawking Warned About the Perils of Artificial Intelligence – Yet AI Gave him a Voice. *The Conversation*, March 16, 2018, http://theconversation.com/ stephen-hawking-warned-about-the-perils-of-artificial-intelligence-yet-ai-gave-him-a-voice-93416.

Schwartz, P., & Ogilvy, J. A. Plotting Your Scenarios. *Learning from the Future: Competitive Foresight Scenarios*, 1998, 57–80.

Shell, Scenarios: www.shell.com/home/content/aboutshell/our_strategy/shell_global_sce narios/scenarios_explorers_guide/; About Us: https://www.shell.com/about-us.html.

Silberg, J., & Manyika, J. Tackling Bias in Artificial Intelligence (and in Humans). *McKinsey Global Institute*, June 2019, www.mckinsey.com/featured-insights/artificial-intelligence/ tackling-bias-in-artificial-intelligence-and-in-humans.

Stevens, M. Orica's Digital Drive to 21st Century Blasting. *Australian Financial Review*, January 2, 2018, www.afr.com/business/oricas-digital-drive-to-21st-century-blasting-20171229-h0bcf0.

Stevens, M. Orica Harvests Calderon's Technology Hunch. *Australian Financial Review*, July 31, 2019, www.afr.com/companies/manufacturing/orica-harvests-calderon-s-technology-hunch-20190730-p52c7s.

Strategic Management Institute (SMI). London Conference, www.smiknowledge.com.

Strategic Management Institute (SMI). Survey on Strategic Management Practices Conducted in Conjunction with Swinburne University in 2013 Unpublished. Copies are Available on Request by Emailing the SMI, smi@smiknowledge.com.

Sysco Annual Report 2019, http://investors.sysco.com/~/media/Files/S/Sysco-IR/documents/annual-reports/2019%20Annual%20Report%20FINAL.pdf.

Sysco At a Glance 2019, www.sysco.com/dam/Sysco/Homepage/at-a-glance-9-18-19.pdf.

Sysco, Reference for Business, Company History Index 2019, www.referenceforbusiness.com/history2/10/SYSCO-Corporation.html.

Toyota, the official blog of Toyota GB, Andon, website 2016, https://blog.toyota.co.uk/andon-toyota-production-system.

Uber: About Us, www.uber.com/au/en/about/.

Wack, P. Scenarios: Uncharted Waters Ahead. *Harvard Business Review*, September–October 1985.

Waldmeir, P. Ford Profits Halve in 2018 as Losses in China and Europe bite Detroit Carmaker Continues Overhaul of Struggling Overseas Operations. *Financial Times*, Chicago, January 24, 2019 https://www.ft.com/content/bdde8468-1f4e-11e9-b126-46fc3ad87c65.

Waters, R. Tesla Posts Deeper than Expected Loss as Profit Margins Fall. *Financial Review*, San Francisco, July 25, 2019, https://www.ft.com/content/b2dbf430-ae58-11e9-8030-530adfa879c2.

Wetselaar, M., Fuels of the Future, https://www.shell.com/media/speeches-and-articles/2019/fuels-of-the-future.html, 2019.

Whittington, R., Cailluet, L., & Yakis-Douglas, B. Opening Strategy: Evolution of a Precarious Profession. *British Journal of Management*, 22, 2011, 531–544.

Wikimedia. 2019, https://www.wikimedia.org/.

WRAP, WRAP and the circular economy, what is a circular economy? 2020, http://www.wrap.org.uk/about-us/about/wrap-and-circular-economy.

Index